A Guide to 95

The First Alternative Windows Book

Credits

Copyright @ 1997 by John Whelan

All rights reserved. Printed in Canada

ISBN 0-89716-601-9

LCC #95-070360

01.0126

Publisher:

Peanut Butter Publishing

226 Second Ave. W.

Seattle, WA 98119

www.pbpublishing.com

Editor: Kathy Markham

Technical Editor: John Whelan

Illustrator: Rick Simpson

Cover Designer: David Pelcyger

Back cover concept: John Whelan

Test Readers: Ben Sims, Tim Whelan, Cephas Bushuyu, Steve Roper Scott Whelan, Ken Blackmon, Julie Dahlem, Gunnar Magnenat, Lee Mullen, Steve Jones, Jason Hall and Jim Whelan (listed in order of their contribution)

Trademarks throughout this book have adapted the capitalization style used by the manufacturer or have been appropriately capitalized to distinguish them from descriptive terms.

Every effort has been made to supply complete and accurate information. However, the author and publisher assumes no responsibility for its use, nor for any infringement of the intellectual property rights of third parties which could result from such use.

Microsoft and Windows are trademarks of Microsoft Corporation.

Any statements said on the behalf of Microsoft are only opinions based on the company's past behavior.

Please email any comments or corrections to jwhelan@wolfenet.com.

Acknowledgments

My publisher told me, when I get to the Acknowledgments page, to make sure I thank everyone. However, first and foremost, I want to thank him. Without him, this book would only exist in my mind. (Actually most of it was pulled out of thin air, just kidding).

I also need to thank my editor, Kathy. She did a great job, especially since my writing skills are probably the worse she has ever encountered.

Many thanks to my friend and illustrator, Rick. With out his help, this book would have lacked a lot of character and not to mention, would have probably been done entirely in MSWORD.

I want to thank all my test readers; Ben, Tim, Cephas, Scott, Steve, Ken, Lee, Julie (the only female test reader), Gunnar, Steve and Jason. Besides the boring details, many of them had to endure the material that wasn't printed!

In addition, I need to thank all my friends, coworkers and family members for putting up with me. I freely admit, I was no fun, boring and stressed-out most of the time; and this was before I even started writting my book.

As for the rest, I want to thank, in no particular order or relevance; Adobe for creating PageMaker (or as I call it, PageSaver); Microsoft for developing Windows and almost hiring me; Hewlett-Packard for designing the best printers in the world; the Exchange for buying the best printers in the world; and Seafirst National Bank for loaning me the money I needed to write this book.

In conclusion, I want to thank everyone whom contributed to this book, knowingly or not. This includes all the people who inspired, encouraged or motivated me into putting my thoughts and ideas down on paper. I am very fortunate to be surrounded by such an abundant amount of positive people!

About the Author, Me

Hello, my name is John and I was born in Seattle, Washington; during the late sixties. I received my education locally and had my first encounter with a computer while still in grade school.

My early experiences with computers revolved mostly around games, which continued well into college. After graduating from Pacific Lutheran Univerity with a Bachelor's degree in Computer Science, I began to take computers much more seriously. I realized the important impact they would have, not only in the business world, but in every aspect of life.

After college, I went to work for some local software companies. During these years, I moved quickly from company to company feeding my appetite for experience. I worked for Aldus (now, known as Adobe), providing technical support for PageMaker. In addition, I worked for IBM as a field engineer and did some testing for Microsoft. These early years were a very busy time for me and my knowledge of computers consummated to a more commercial level.

In fact, I learned a lot more about computers from these jobs, than I had in school. They did not have classes on Windows at Pacific Lutheran. So all my PC skills were acquired after college. It is these skills which I believe are in high demand today.

Currently, I work at the Exchange as a System Engineer. I provide technical support to field engineers and help maintain a local network of ATMs (Automatical Teller Machines) which stretch across more than 6 states. Though this job keeps me very busy, I still find time to indulge some of my passions.

A couple of years ago, one of these passions was to write a computer book. In the past, I had always used computer books when I was in need of assistance. Though many of these books were excellent guides, a thought kept crossing my mind; "I could do that!"

I believed I could write a book, more human and helpful than those I had seen in the past. Though most computer books written today have greatly relaxed their vocabulary, when compared to computer books of the past, they still have not quite hit the spot.

I feel, many users want to read a book which is directed towards beginners, but they do not want to be treated like children in the process. They want a guide for <u>smart</u> people, who do not necessarily have a lot of experience with computers. A few years ago, I was a lot like one of these users. So, I understand the conflicts and realized my book would have to be written for these kind of users.

A Guide to 95 is a collection of my skills, experiences and thoughts about Windows 95. It covers a lot more information about computers in general, than just Windows. The reason behind this, is one day I believe Windows will cover a lot more than just computer screens.

Enjoy my book, John

Table of Contents

The Introduction...1

1 Introduction 3
    What is Windows? 4
    What is Windows 95? 7
    Why use Windows 95? 11
    Why use this book? 12

2 Installation 17
    Your Computer 18
    Installing Windows 95 20
    What is a Startup Disk? 27

3 Getting Started. 29
    Working with windows 30
    Resizing windows 34
    Working with the Menu bar. 36
    What are Properties? 38

The Windows 95 Road Map..41

4 The Taskbar...43

      How to use the Taskbar.................................45
      The Start Button.......................................47
      Programs...48
      Documents..49
      Settings...50
      Working with Printers..................................51
      Setting up the Taskbar.................................53
      Finding Files..56
      Help!..57
      Run and Shut Down......................................58

5 My Computer and The Windows Explorer.........................59

      My Computer..60
      Moving files around My Computer........................62
      Renaming files...63
      Deleting files...64
      Making Shortcuts.......................................65
      Deleting Shortcuts.....................................66
      The Windows Explorer...................................67
      Moving files in the Windows Explorer...................68

6 The Recycle Bin..71

      How to use the Recycle Bin.............................72
      Working with the Recycle Bin...........................75

7 The Control Panel..79

      The Control Panel......................................80
      Add New Hardware.......................................81
      Add/Remove Programs....................................82
      Date/Time..84
      Display..85

	Fonts	.86
	Internet	.88
	Joystick	.89
	Keyboard	.90
	Networks, Modems, Mail and Fax	.92
	Mouse	.93
	Multimedia	.93
	Passwords	.93
	Printers	.94
	Regional Settings	.95
	Sounds	.96
	System	.99

8 The Display 103

    Background 104
    Screen Savers 108
    The Appearance 111
    Settings 113

9 The Mouse 115

    What is a mouse? 116
    Working with a mouse 118
    The Mouse Properties window 120
    "Clicking the keyboard" 124

Working with Windows 95..........................127

10 "I want my Windows 3.1 back!"..........129
- Getting Back the old File Manager..........130
- Using the File Manager and Program Manager..........134
- Where is My Task List?..........137

11 The Ten Pack..........139
- The Ten Pack..........140
- Calculator..........142
- Calendar..........143
- Cardfile..........145
- Character Map..........148
- Clipboard Viewer..........150
- HyperTerminal..........151
- Notepad..........154
- Paint..........156
- Phone Dialer..........158
- Wordpad..........161

12 The Utilities..........163
- What is a Utility?..........164
- Microsoft Backup..........164
- Scandisk..........168
- Compressing Data..........170
- Disk Defragmenter..........172
- System Monitor..........174

13 The Games..........175
- Solitaire..........176
- FreeCell..........178
- Hearts..........180
- Minesweeper..........182
- Top Secret Minesweeper Hints..........184

14 Multimedia. 187
    The CD Player 188
    Controlling the Volume 190
    Customizing CDs 193
    Customizing the CD Player 195
    Using the Media player and Sound Recorder 197

15 Sending and Receiving Faxes 199
    What is a fax? 200
    What is a modem? 201
    Creating a Cover Page 203
    Creating and Sending Faxes 205
    Receiving Faxes 208

16 The Microsoft Network 211
    On-line Networks 212
    The Internet 213
    What Microsoft has to offer 214
    e-mail 220

17 Plug and Play 223
    Plug and Play in the Past 224
    Plug and Play 225
    What's next? 229

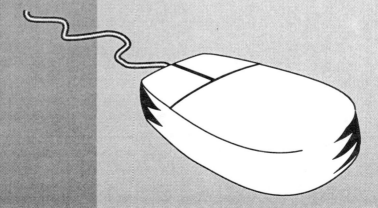

The Windows 95 Wrap-Up..231

18 Tricks, Hints and Traps 233
- Windows Tricks 234
- Helpful Hints...247
- Deadly Traps...251
- Stopping run away DOS Programs.........................253

19 The Windows 95 Art Gallery 255
- The Gallery 256
- The Icon Room 257
- The Windows Showcase 263
- Microangelo 264
- PCasso 266
- RAMbrandt 268
- Whelanardo da Vinci 270
- The Exit 271

20 Life Outside of Windows 95 273
- 32-bit Processing 274
- Microsoft Plus and the Desktop 276
- The Microsoft Agents 279
- The Internet Explorer 282
- Windows 95 inside and out 285

The Index 287

Introduction

CHAPTER 1

I have a great idea. Let's do away with computer books which intimidate and restrict people. Instead create one which explores options in plain English with a unique approach. It would be easy to understand, while not directed toward dummies.

Well, here it is! A book designed to start you off on the right foot with Windows. So, if you are new to Windows or just upgrading your system, I believe you will find this book extremely helpful, as well as entertaining.

What is Windows?

Although it's packaged the same as other software titles, Windows 95 itself is very different. As an operating system, it is the central piece of software which runs your personal computer and allows you to interact with it. Windows 95 takes this role still further by including a friendlier interface, some additional programs, as well as lots new features.

Windows was first released back in 1985. Since then, this revolutionary operating system has grown to become the most widely used software in the world. If Microsoft had a signature song, Windows would be it. Through the success of this operating system, Microsoft has achieved an 80% (or better) market share. Customers have shown they are more interested in usability rather than functionality. After all, what is the point of a good computer if it is too difficult to use or understand.

But, before I jump into Windows, I think you should know a little more about the history behind it. Long before there ever was a concept called Windows, an earlier operating system ruled the industry. This operating system was called PC-DOS and was originally designed by Microsoft for IBM personal computers. IBM chose Microsoft to write the software which would provide all the initial instructions for its personal computers. This software was maintained on a disk (the word DOS actually means "**D**isk **O**perating **S**ystem") and was loaded every time a computer was turned on. After these instructions were loaded, it wasn't necessary to reload them again, as long as the computer stayed on.

The operating system soon developed into an important part of the personal computer and Microsoft had to continue to improve upon its design, in order to keep up with the speed of technology. Although DOS was very powerful, it was also very dull and unsympathetic, mainly because it was command driven.

By the early eighties it was obvious a more inviting operating system had to be designed. Since most PCs were already set-up with DOS, Microsoft decided to make a graphical extension for its DOS users. So, instead of designing an entirely new operating system, they continued to develop DOS and provided it with a secondary software package, which would be more appealing. This package is now known as Windows.

Introduction

The first version of Windows, Windows 1.0, was delivered back in late 1985. It was a new concept with many new features, including an entirely new simplistic interface. In addition to its layout, Windows took advantage of "point and click" reasoning and allowed its users total freedom of the screen. It also allowed users to run multiple programs and switch among them without pausing. This feature was not available for past DOS users. In DOS, only one program could be executed at a time.

Unfortunately for Windows, the hardware at the time was very limited and had difficulty supporting such an immense operating system. Because of this, Microsoft's new design had a tough time getting the public's attention.

However, by the time Microsoft shipped version 3.0, the market had sweetened up to the idea of Windows. Most personal computers had better processors and could now afford to handle much more memory. With its release in May of 1990, Windows 3.0 became an overnight success. This most recent version of Windows was less demanding on hardware and more productive with its results. Soon to follow was the release of Windows 3.1.

Because of its simple interface and crude effectiveness, Windows 3.1 attracted many new users. People liked the idea of making things happen with a click of a mouse. With the popularity and success of Windows 3.1, Microsoft became the world's largest software developer. It sold millions of copies and helped reinforce the software industry. Unfortunately, as effective and efficient as it was, Windows 3.1, itself was in need of an upgrade and this paved the way for Windows 95 (and this book).

What is an upgrade? An upgrade is like a face-lift. When a particular program is successful, many times the program out lasts its original intent. People begin to use it in situations it may not have been designed for, thereby necessitating an upgrade.

What is an update? An update is like an upgrade, only on a smaller scale. When a program is developed, some bugs may be exposed when it is used in certain situations. Then the program needs to be updated.

What is Windows 95?

Windows 95, formally code named *Chicago*, is the newest version of Windows. It is a 32-bit operating system which emulates a multi-tasking environment. In non-technical terms, Windows 95 is the latest operating system from Microsoft which is designed to make computing even easier and better than it has ever been before.

Development began in early 1992 and has been Microsoft's main focus for the last couple of years. After a few delays, the upgrade for Windows 3.1 is finally complete. It is expected to sell 10 million plus copies within the first six months of its release. Although Windows 95 was designed as an upgrade, its features and appearances take on an entirely new look. The list below helps describe some of the differences you will find between Windows 95 and its previous versions.

✓ **The Windows interface.** The Windows 95 interface is a lot different from its earlier versions. Microsoft has taken out all those confusing windows inside of windows and replaced them with a more clearer arrangement. Windows 95 has even taken on some Macintosh characteristics, which means it will be easier for past Mac users to convert to Windows.

Figure 1.1
A new interface

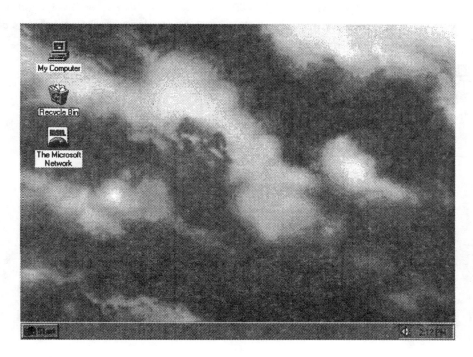

✓ **A New Look**. Once installed, Windows 95 changes the appearance of its menus, windows and title bars. Microsoft added a shinier metallic look to them while decreasing the size of their fonts. This makes the screen look more professional, while at the same time, keeping its interface elementary.

Figure 1.2
The old Windows 3.1 Interface

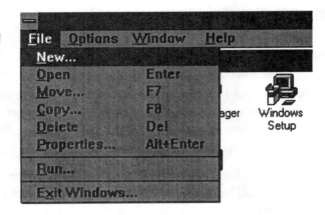

This is the first version of Windows to actually change its physical appearance. Before, the general appearance of Windows had always been relatively constant. Which means after years of development, Microsoft has probably given us a new look that could last longer than the original.

Figure 1.3
The new Windows 95 Interface

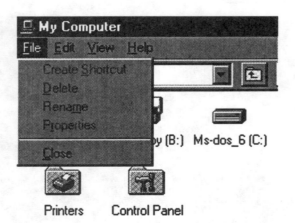

- ✓ **New Windows 95 Features**. Windows 95 includes many new features, foreign to previous Windows users. These features or enhancments are designed to make Windows 95 a more universal program and keep it competitive. Among them is the widely publicized concept, commercially known as *Plug and Play*.

    Plug and Play was created to eliminate all the problems associated with adding new system components; like sound cards, CD-ROMs or modems. This has always been a sore spot for the computer industry, and perhaps someday Plug and Play may help establish some standards.

- ✓ **New Windows 95 Programs**. Along with this new operating system, users will also find many new programs. These programs include; the *Phone Dialer*, *WordPad*, a host of new *games,* as well as others, and are designed to help make Windows 95 into a complete package. When put together, they make Windows into a tool, rather than just an operating system.

- ✓ **Enhanced Windows 3.1 Programs**. Windows 95 still has all of the traditional programs from its earlier generations. However, most of these programs, like Paint Brush, have been touched-up and modernized so they will not become extinct.

- ✓ **Better System Tools**. Windows 95 has improved and increased the number of system tools. They include a *CD-Player*, a *fax machine* and a larger number of *utilities*. All these tools come standard with Windows 95, regardless of whether or not you have the hardware to support them.

- ✓ **Farewell to DOS**. Windows 95 no longer needs DOS in order to operate. This means you can still run *DOS applications* inside of Windows, but you no longer have to mess with DOS as an operating system (*yeah!*).

    Microsoft has been trying to squeeze DOS out of the picture for years. Now, with Windows 95, let's hope its disappearance will be noticed, but not unused.

- ✓ **32-bit processing**. Although computers, themselves have had the ability to handle a 32-bit architecture for years, it has always been the operating system (DOS in particular) which held them back. With the arrival of Windows 95, that is about to change. Unlike earlier versions of Windows, Windows 95 can handle both 16 and 32 bits programs.

- ✓ **Nametags instead of Icons.** Although there are a few icons still remaining on its desktop, the majority of programs in Windows 95 now use nametags instead. Nametags can hold more information about a program, then icons can and nametags only require one click!

- ✓ **Other changes.** In addition, you will notice many other differences between Windows 95 and its earlier versions. However, as a rule of thumb, Microsoft has made this version easier to use.

Why Use Windows 95?

It seems like only yesterday, Windows 3.1 was redefining the high technology industry. Yet this version is already outdated. Chances are by the time you fully understand Windows 95, it too will be outdated. With technology advancing so quickly, even its users can't keep up with it. Truth is, as long as the technology is available, its users will always be scrabbling to keep up with it. This is very clear in the PC market, where today's Pentium workhorses are 10 times faster than computers developed only a couple of years ago.

In the high technology market, upgrades are very common. These upgrades frequently provide a means of prolonging a program's life. However, the degree of an upgrade's modification can range quite drastically. Some upgrades are minor and can easily be overlooked, while others are more momentous. In most cases, the extent of the upgrade is often mirrored by the program's overall success. Now, when it comes to Windows 95, this upgrade is very crucial. In many ways, it will redefine Windows and the entire high technology industry. So, you can bet a lot of research went into its development.

Not to mention, Windows 95 offers unlimited potential. Because of its power and completeness, it can thrust any personal computer far beyond their previous performance levels. It also has an elegant interface, lots of real value and is tons of fun.

Windows 95 is a great platform for beginners, because its layout is set up to be open and inviting. It also has some Macintosh characteristics which makes it easier for past Mac users to convert.

Micsosoft is even using this upgrade to promote itself as well as other newer products, like the Microsoft Network and Internet Explorer. With combinations like these, it is the users who triumph.

In addition, considering Windows has achieved a world audience, Microsoft has been forced to make its upgrade, Windows 95, into a complete universal program. Since it will be used in homes as well as in the work place, and distributed to a wide range of customers, Windows 95 will allow its users learn at home and then apply their experiences at work and all over the world.

In conclusion, Windows 95 is a great and powerful operating system. It comes from a lengthy heritage of operating systems and like its predecessors, it will no doubt change the computer industry forever.

Why use this Book?

This book, <u>A Guide to 95</u> was written for PC users everywhere. It is designed to introduce them to the Windows 95 environment without having to make them stumble over the terminology first. With its unique approach, this book makes Windows 95 painless and fun.

This book was mainly written to offer assistance and help users learn how to maneuver around Windows 95 without any worries. Since this is a new operating system, I understand its layout may not be as simple as it seems, especially to new users.

Many of the "buttons" and "windows" in Windows 95 may seem bewildering if not redundant, mainly because most of them are. Many buttons do the same thing, and many windows look the same. This all adds up to the confusion of Windows. Even if Windows 95 doesn't baffle you, it will no doubt shock you. Experienced or not, Windows 95 is a new program full of new surprises.

Now, when it comes to assistance, Windows 95 does provide its users with two included alternatives. First, there is the user manual. This is a 95-page book, designed to offer printed assistance and an overall introduction of the operating system. The manual is very brief and does not go into much detail, therefore doesn't offer much assistance either.

The second alternative is the Help program within Windows 95. Help programs, in general, are very popular today and usually compensate for hundreds (if not thousands) of pages of text. They offer immediate help with little or no effort. However, they also can be intimidating and confusing for new users. After all, if you are having problems in Windows, using a Windows Help program to assist you would be like getting assistance from the problem-maker itself.

Aside from these alternatives, there are books like mine. Computer books offer much more than their computer equivalent. They provide great examples as well as unrivaled human experiences. In addition, they are also very portable and work even when the computer is turned off.

Introduction

In the past, computer books have gotten a bad reputation, because they often appear to be too confusing. They would use words like; *distribution media, standard output* and *modules*. This often made these kind of books more confusing than helpful. In addition, some of these book never seemed to be written by humans; they had few examples and almost no humor.

However, my book is not one of these! My book uses lots of simple terminology and easy-to-follow examples. It was written in your language, a plain dialect originating from the suburbs of Seattle, on a computer much like the one you may be using; by a mortal much like yourself (only smarter and better-looking).

A Guide to 95 is a book which will aid rookies and assist veterans. It will clear up any clouds around this new operating system, and provide its readers with valuable information.

This book includes many pictures and diagrams of Windows 95. I feel, when it comes to Windows, seeing is learning. In this book, I use as few technical terms as possible. However, there are some words which must be used. You can't explain Windows without using some high-tech jargon. So if you happen to be unaware of or uncomfortable with this terminology, let me take this chance to bring you up to speed.

Technical Term	The Meaning...
Application	Any program (sometimes referred to as an **App.**).
Bear	Australian for beer.
Executable	A run-able file, usually ends with .**exe**, .**com** or .**bat**. For example, install.exe or calc.exe.
CD-ROM	Data stored on a compact disk in a READ only format.
Clipboard	A temporary holding spot for text and graphical data, which is universal among other programs.
CPU	Central Processing Unit is the main internal chip which is responsible for the speed and overall performance of a computer.
"Ctrl-Alt-Del"	Kills or stops (not deletes) any currently running program after pressing this combination of keys. This is only meant to be used in extreme cases.
Format	A guideline for structure of data.

Default	The selection which is taken if the user does not actively select one.
Diskette	An external medium used to store data on. Usually available in many different sizes and formats.
Dialog box	A pop-up window which provides information.
DOS	An early operating system for PCs, sometimes referred to as **MS-DOS** or **PC-DOS**.
Driver	Internal software which connects external devices.
File	A location within a computer used to store data. This can include programs, documents, pictures or almost anything...
Font	A type or character style. Me, For *Example*.
GUI	A **Graphical User Interface** is essentially the way Windows presents itself to its users (i.e. through graphics).
Hard Drive	A physical device within a computer where information is stored permently.
Icon	A graphical representation of data (or a command).
Meg	Or Mega-byte is a unit of measure for memory. 1 MB = 1,000,000 bytes
Modem	A device which allows computers to communicate with each other; or in other words, a computer phone.
Multimedia	The combination of 2 or more mediums, usually mixing pictures and sounds.
Multi-tasking	The ability to run many programs at once (i.e. to walk and chew gum at the same time).
PC	The abbreviation for the personal computer.
Program	A collection of data (or files) which completes a certain task.
Program Group	A collection of programs.
RAM	**Random Access Memory**, or commonly known as short term memory, is the memory which the CPU is <u>actively</u> using.
ROM	**Read Only Memory**, or permanent memory, is the memory which is retained after a computer is turned off.
Scroll bar	A bar located on the side or bottom of windows, which allows users to view entire sections of the screen.

Toolbar	A collection of buttons designed to make common features of a program easier to access.
WYSIWYG	Pronounced like "wizzy wig", it means: *what you see is what you get*.
Wallpaper	The background image in Windows.

Now that we have the terminology out of the way, let's get down to business. I have written this book to be very easy to follow. It has been separated into four sections to help you navigate through Windows 95. Here is a break-down and brief description of each section:

① **The Introduction**. This is the section you are currently reading, and it is divided into two major parts. The first part introduces you to the Windows 95 environment and describes the general outline of this book. The second part will discuss how to install Windows 95. It will also help you set-up your system and describes some basic concepts surrounding Windows. If you have a good amount of Windows experience, you may "unofficially" skip this section if you want to.

② **The Windows 95 Road Map**. In this section, I take an in-depth look at the Windows 95 interface and help guide you through this radical operating system. By explaining all the different parts and components of Windows 95, I help you get the most out of it. The road map section goes basically piece by piece through the Windows 95 environment.

③ **Working with Windows 95**. In this section, I illustrate all the new features of Windows 95 and show how to use them. After all, what is the point of upgrading, if you don't understand how to use its new features. I also spend some time clarifying the differences between the early versions of Windows and Windows 95. In this section, there will be a lot of "hands-on" descriptions and examples.

④ **The Windows 95 Wrap-up**. By the time you reach this section, Windows 95 should make sense. You should be able to dance around its environment and use its new features. So, in this section, I spend time showing some Windows' tricks, hints and traps; as well as other ways to showcase this unique operating system.

> * There are many different ways to utilize this book. Some readers may skip from topic to topic, while others may read it straight through. How ever you decide to use it, make sure it does not go unused. After all, an unused computer book is usually only inches away from an unused computer.

Installation

CHAPTER 2

This chapter explains how to correctly install Windows 95 and initially customize for your system. In general, installation is a routine which naturally should only be done once in a Windows lifetime. However, since re-installing Windows 95 is one of the most popular remedies for many system failures; this routine which should only be done once, is far more popular than other one time acts. Therefore, it is good idea to get as familiar with this process as possible.

Your Computer

In general, computers are made up of many complicated parts with each part playing an important role. It is difficult to pin point each and every component of a computer. Yet, there are at least three parts which all users should be aware of. They are the **CPU**, **RAM** and **Hard drive**. These three components usually define strength and price of any computer.

RAM or Random Access Memory is also called *short term memory*, because it is the memory you loose when the computer is turned off. Memory is basically pliable sectors on a chip which are used for storing information.

RAM is usually specified as *RAM chips* or *SIM chips*. The difference between these chips is the amount of memory they can hold. In general, Sim chips have a better design and can hold more memory than RAM chips. They are also more efficient and expandable.

Windows has always been quite a memory hog (for lack of a better word), making memory an asset which you may need to invest in. Most PCs have at least 2 - 4 Megs of RAM. This was the bare minimum for any previous versions of Windows. However, in order for Windows 95 to run smoothly, its users will have to have at least 4 - 8 Megs of RAM.

If you were purchasing a new computer today, I would recommend at least 8 Megs of RAM or 16 Megs, if you could afford it. If you already own a computer, which is under-staffed in RAM. You can always buy more RAM, since it is not too expensive considering all the technical aspects aspects surrounding it. The rule of thumb with RAM is, buy as much as you can afford at the present time; then if you need more, you can buy it later.

Figure 2.1
A SIM chip

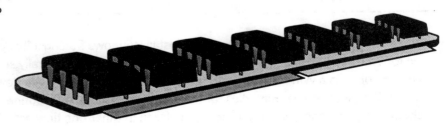

Another key ingredient of a computer is the **Hard Drive**. This is the place where all the information is stored permanently. It is a lot like a warehouse or a parking garage for the files on a computer. It is where data is stored, even when the data is not in use.

The amount of room which a hard drive is allowed to use is commonly known as *hard drive space*. Unlike RAM, which fluctuates heavily depending upon the computer's usage, hard drive space remains relatively constant. Hard drive space only changes when programs or files are added to a system, regardless if they are used or not.

Generally, Windows 95 takes up a fair amount of hard drive space, which is to be expected since it is a rather large program. However, drive space is not the biggest concern when it comes to installing Windows.

One of the biggest concerns when it comes to Windows 95 is power! Because Windows 95 is so advanced, it takes a rather powerful computer to handle it. The power in most personal computers comes from the combination of The CPU and its RAM. The CPU mainly provides the speed while the RAM supplies the strength.

Some older systems may encounter problems running Windows 95 causing it to run abnormally slow or not at all. The table outlined below is designed to give you an idea about which system works best with Windows 95.

System	RAM	Performance
286	2 - 4 RAM	Sorry, this system is not powerful enough to run Windows 95; need to upgrade system.
386SX	4 RAM	Sorry, this system may have problems with Windows 95; may need to upgrade.
386DX	4 - 8 RAM	This system will run Windows 95, just barely.
486(any)	8 - 16 RAM	This system will run Windows 95 without any problems. Speed will depend on RAM.
Pentium	8 - 32 RAM	This system will run Windows 95 like a champ.

Installing Windows 95

The retail version of Windows 95 is packaged in three different ways; as a CD-ROM upgrade, as a diskette upgrade or as the complete non-Windows version. All packages include the most current version of Windows 95. However, depending upon what your computer can support, will help you decide which package to purchase.

The **CD-ROM upgrade** is designed for users currently running Windows 3.0 or later. In order to use this upgrade, your computer must have a CD-ROM drive. The CD-ROM upgrade is the best way to purchase Windows 95. First of all, it is the least expensive. Furthermore, when it comes to installation, the CD takes half as long as the diskettes do. Not to mention, with the CD, you do not have to swap a lot of diskettes in and out of the computer.

The **diskette upgrade** is mainly designed for users currently running Windows 3.0 or later, who do not own a CD-ROM drive. Since every computer has some sort of disk drive, this upgrade is suitable for anyone.

The **complete non-Windows** version of Windows 95 is only available in diskettes and is the most expensive. Though, its name is a little mis-leading, since every package contains the most complete version of Windows 95, regardless. What makes this package different, is it's set up for non-Windows users.

Since CD-ROMs are more mechanical than disk drives, they tend to break down more often. This could leave most users high-and-dry when it comes to re-installation. In these cases, it would be a good idea to have the complete non-Windows version. This version can usually save anyone from the most severe of problems.

* The picture of the retail version of Windows 95 was reprinted with permission from Microsoft Corporation

Installation

After purchasing Windows 95, you may be in for a little surprise. Windows 95 is quite different then previous versions. The box it comes in may look familiar; but once you have broken that plastic, you will soon discover a few changes.

Luckily for you, all those horror stories about installations gone wrong do not apply with Windows 95. The installation of Windows 95 is relatively painless and easy. By creating a program or as Microsoft likes to put it a "wizard", Windows 95 virtually installs itself automatically for you. Finding this program (wizard) and starting it, is only tricky part about the installation.

In general, it is easier to install Windows 95 then it is to explain how. So instead of giving you the full blown details, I'll just start you off on the right foot. You won't believe how easy it is.

- ☑ First, turn on your computer.

- ☑ Start up Windows. In some computers, Windows will start up automatically. In others, you may have to type the command "**win**" at the DOS prompt.

- ☑ If you haven't already done so, remove the Windows CD from its package and put it in your CD-ROM drive. If you have the diskette version, place the first diskette in the disk drive and leave the others close by your computer and arrange numerically.

- ☑ By using the mouse, go to the Menu bar and click on the word **File**. Drag the mouse pointer down to the **RUN...** option and double-click on it.

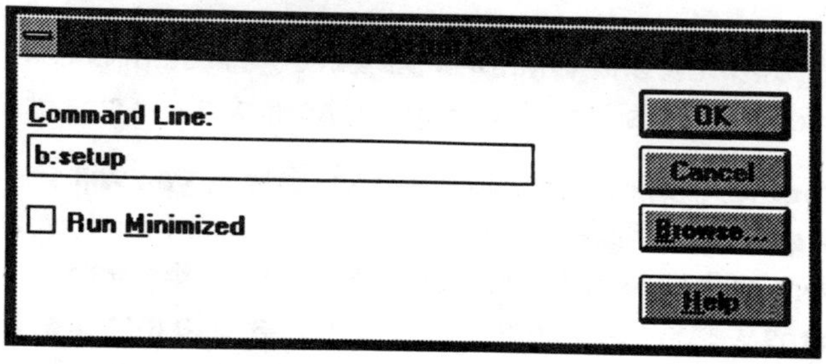

Figure 2.2
The Run dialog box

- ☑ Now, type "**x:setup**" and hit return key. The letter **x** represents the drive which Windows is being copied from. On most computers, it will either be an **A** (for diskette) or **D** (for CD-ROM).

- ☑ From here on, Windows 95 will basically install itself. Simply, watch the screen and follow the directions. If you are using diskettes, you will need to change them every time Windows prompts you. In addition, don't be surprised if you are asked to skip a diskette. Those missed diskettes will be used later.

- ☑ The first display you will see looks something like the picture below. Notice Microsoft's new installation wallpaper, upon completing installation, you get to keep it for your screen.

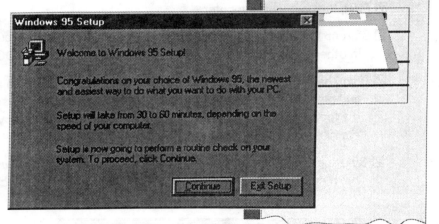

Figure 2.3
The Setup Interface

- ☑ Click on **Continue**, and Windows 95 will do a system check. This process takes a few seconds, depending upon the speed and size of the computer.

- ☑ After Windows 95 finishes checking the system, you will see **Microsoft's Software License Agreement**. Please take some time to read it. Use the scroll bars at the side of the screen to see all of the agreement. As if technical terms weren't bad enough, now you have to interpret legal terms as well. At this point, you can either click on **Yes** and agree to Microsoft's deal, or you can click on **No** and Windows 95 will not be installed. Those are the rules of the game, plain and simple.

INSTALLATION 23

☑ Within a few minutes, the Windows 95 **Setup Wizard** starts up. What is a wizard? A wizard is a Microsoft invention designed to help out novice users. Windows 95 is not the only Microsoft product which has a wizard. wizards are very popular in all of their software.

Figure 2.4
The Setup Wizard

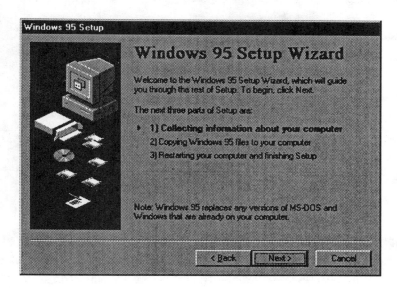

☑ The screen shown above outlines the basic steps for installation. First Windows 95 **collects information** about the system, then **copies its files** and finally does some **cleaning up**. Along the way, you will be asked some important questions.

☑ The first question asked is which directory you want to install Windows 95 in. I strongly recommend leaving it in its default directory, **C:\WINDOWS**. Putting it anywhere else could cause problems and conflict with other programs.

☑ The next window to look out for, is the **Setup Options** window. In this window, you decide how you want Windows 95 installed. You are given four options; *Typical, Compact, Laptop* and *Custom*. The Setup Options window is shown on the next page.

Figure 2.5
The Setup Options window

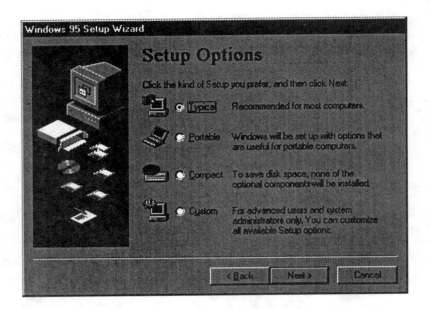

- ☑ The window shown above, gives you the opportunity to select the best layout which matches with your system. This is one feature which makes Windows 95 very flexable. The list below explains each selection;

Typical - This is the most popular and "worry-free" choice. It is at the top of the list for that reason.

Portable - This option is designed for laptop or mobile computers. This option includes lots of useful features for people on the go.

Compact - This option is designed to save drive space. It copies only the minimal amount of files needed. Though, generally it is a good idea to save disk space, this is not the way to do it.

Custom - This option allows users to customize their operating system. Although this option may seem too technical, in reality, it is a lot of fun. It lets users pick which selection of additional Windows programs to include with their installation. Selecting these programs here, will save a lot of time later on.

Figure 2.6
Windows analyzing your computer

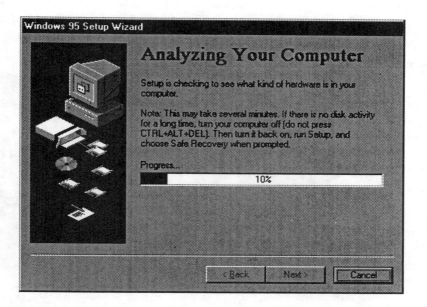

- ☑ After the setup option has been selected, Windows 95 will analyze your entire computer. This process can take 2-3 minutes. It is important to follow Windows' recommendation; which states during this process, if there is no disk activity for a long time, turn your computer off. It strongly recommends not using "Ctrl+Alt+Delete".

- ☑ At some time during the installation process, you will be asked to type in your *name and company*. If you are using Windows 95 for home use, you can type your name in twice (once in the name section and once company section) or leave the company section blank.

- ☑ Subsequently, if you ever make a mistake during the installation of Windows 95, simply click on the **<Back** button in the next window. This will allow you to go back and fix your mistake.

- ☑ At this point Windows is ready to copy all its files on to your computer. So, follow the directions given to you by the Microsoft wizard and you can't go wrong. In fact, the rest of the installation is completed by the wizard.

Figure 2.7
Copying Windows 95

- ☑ As all the files are copies, Windows will provide you with a chart showing the percentage of files it has left to copy. It you are using diskettes, Windows will also prompt you when it is time to interchange them.

- ☑ As the installation nears its end, you will be asked to reset your computer a couple of times. This allows Windows to register all of its updated files with your computer and its new operating system.

What is a Startup Disk?

During the installation of Windows 95, the Microsoft wizard may ask you if you want to make a Startup disk. I recommend making one. A Startup disk is like a back-up disk which only backs up key system files. These files are essential and could be needed when experiencing system problems. By making a Startup disk now, you are protecting yourself later on.

Figure 2.8
Making a Startup disk

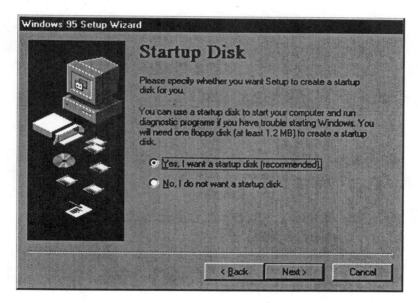

To make a Startup disk, find an old blank disk which is not in use. Make sure you label it as your Startup disk, so you will be able to find it in the future. Insert the disk into your disk drive and follow the wizard's directions.

When Windows 95 has finished making the Startup disk, remove it from the drive and put it somewhere safe and memorable. Because you never know when you might need it again.

Getting Started

CHAPTER 3

It is almost time to start using Windows 95. However before doing so, I want to make sure everyone is comfortable with the Windows environment. Considering the concept of Windows may be foreign to some of my readers, I thought I should include a chapter for the real beginners, mainly concentrating on the fundamentals of Windows. If this seems trivial to you, chances are you're not a real beginner, but instead more of a confused user. In either case, a simple brush up couldn't hurt.

There are certain concepts which are essential to all the versions of Windows, including Windows 95. These concepts are what define the look and feel of the program. Fortunately for its users, the concepts in Windows have not changed much over the years and are still instinctively easy to pick up. They are less technical then one might think and consist more of windows jargon than anything else.

In addition, I believe it is very important for computer users to understand all the aspects of their environment, not to just appreciate their surroundings, but to be able to manipulate their boundaries as well.

Working with windows

If the title "**Working with windows**" caught you off guard, then you might be more fluent in Windows terminology than you think. Because the word "windows", can be a little misleading. It actually has three different definitions. The table below, outlines how the word "windows" is used in this book.

Term	The meaning	How to recognize it
Windows 95 or Windows 3.1	Refers to a particular version of Microsoft's operating system	It will always be capitalized and followed by a number
Windows	Refers to the operating system itself, all versions	It will be capitalized
windows	Refers to an on-screen box	It will be in lower-case

The rest of this chapter refers to the last definition of word **windows**. It is because of these windows, Microsoft's operating system is such a success. They have grown to be a very familiar landmark and continue to provide structure in today's technology.

Although these windows may appear to be simple and quite harmless. In their own way, they have revolutionalized the computer industry and forever altered its path; mainly, because these windows can transform confusing and complex equations into a simple environment, which we can understand and use.

A window is basically a box, displayed on a screen. It has few distractions and possesses a "childlike" appearance. It can contain almost anything. It can hold information, programs or even other windows. It can be nearly any size and can be placed anywhere on or off the screen.

A window can be found in any Windows program, not just in the operating system. It is a fundamental building block and everything either starts or ends with a window. Although these windows themselves do not appear to do much, they cannot be overlooked since they provide the Windows environment with **structure**.

An operating system, like Windows 95, works by lending its windows to other programs, just like a nation distributes its currency. It allows other programs to go ahead and use its windows, as long as these programs follow the rules set up by the operating system.

A window is the main component which defines all Windows programs and makes them stand apart from the other programs. This is why a Windows program will look quite different than a DOS program, even if they are both running on the same computer.

Some examples of windows can be seen on the next page:

Figure 3.1
A typical program window

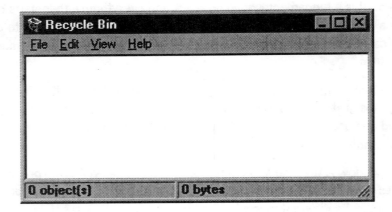

Figure 3.2
A typical informational window

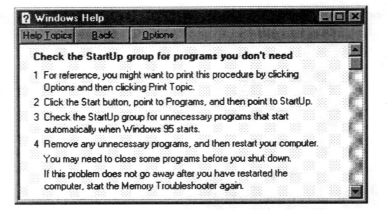

Figure 3.3
A typical confirmation window

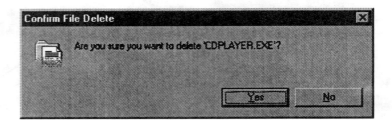

The windows in Windows 95 are the same as they were in previous versions; they only look a little different. So, if you knew how to use them then, you won't have any problems using them now. However, if you haven't used windows before or still haven't quite figured them out, the rest of this chapter should help you a lot. To begin with, let's look at a typical window.

Figure 3.4
A window in Windows 95

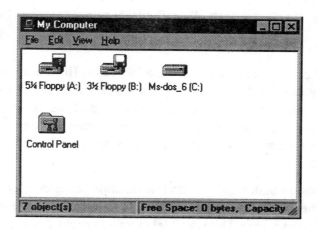

The window shown above is one example of a window. As you can see, it is quite empty and very plain. It has a title with a little icon on it, a menu bar and some buttons in the right hand corner (used for resizing). These are common properties of windows, but are not always necessary. There are only three required properties a window **must** have. They are:

① A **title**
② A particular **function** or task
③ A **close button**, or resizing buttons

The **title** gives a brief description about the window. It is always located at the top of the window and sometimes includes a picture, or an icon with it. Needless to say, the title is a good place to look at if you are lost or confused about which window you are in. If a window is active, then its title bar will darken, otherwise it will remain unchanged.

Every window also has a purpose. Some windows may provide information, while others perform certain tasks. In any case, a window always does something, whether you know it or not. Consequently, anytime a window is opened, or started, it is expected to fulfill a task.

Resizing windows

The last requirement for windows, are the resizing buttons. These are those little buttons at the top right hand side of every window. They are responsible for positioning the window on the screen. Each window frequently has a few buttons or may contain just one. The buttons themselves have different symbols on them to help distinguish them from each other. The table below describes the most common ones:

This button **closes** the window it is attached to. This means when you click it, the window and everything in it stops executing and it is removed from the screen. This button is <u>always</u> visible, and allows the user to close any application at any time. (*This would be the button you would click if you opened a window by mistake and wanted to close it without causing any damage.*)

The **minimize** button causes windows to shrink considerably. By clicking it, the window the button is attached to is placed on the Taskbar, instead of on the screen. This way it takes up less room. Suppose you want to clear up the screen. The minimize button would be a useful tool, since it can hide windows in the Taskbar. It doesn't close or stop them, it just moves them out of the way for later use.

The **maximize** button makes the window the button is attached to increase in size to fit the <u>entire</u> screen. When this button is clicked, it causes the window to enlarge, while all the other windows on the screen become hidden.

This button is only visible after the maximize has been chosen. It is used to resize the enlarged window back to its initial size. Think of it as an **"undo"** button for the maximize button.

The **help** button is designed to answer any questions about a particular window. When clicked on, it starts the Microsoft Help program and automatically goes to the correct section in the program which deals with the subject you need help on. This button is not very common in windows, since there are other more efficient ways of getting help, like by pressing the **F1** key!

Not all of the buttons described in this book appear on every window. Some windows may be missing a few buttons. This doesn't mean they are defective, it only means, the missing buttons weren't needed. In fact, the only necessary button for a window is the **Close** button.

Another way to adjust the size of a window is to do it manually, by using the mouse. If you want to enlarge a window, place the mouse cursor on the boundaries of that window and pull it out toward the edges of the screen. Remember to hold the left mouse button down while doing so.

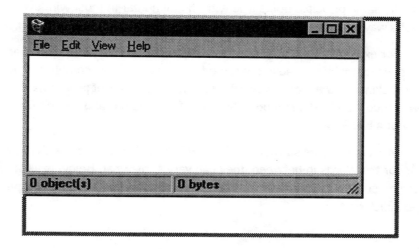

Figure 3.5
Enlarging a window using the mouse

To reduce the size of a window, place the mouse cursor on the boundaries of the window and push it inward toward the center of the screen. Remember to hold the left mouse button down while doing so.

You can resize a window to any particular dimension you want and if you grow weary of resizing them, you can move them as well. Because moving a window is a lot like moving the mouse cursor, except in this case the cursor is holding something. To move a window, grab it from the top and pull it along with the mouse. If a window doesn't seem to pick up, try grabbing it from its **title**.

Working with the Menu bar

Most windows have an arrangement of options available to use, either comprising of push-buttons or a full scale menu bar. These options are usually located at the top of the window, just below its title. They are very consistent throughout many Windows programs and quite popular.

The options on the menu bar are available for you to use and operate much like a menu at a restaurant, however instead of meals, they provide features of a program. Like the menu at a restaurant, frequent customers may not always use it. The same principle holds true with the menu bar in most windows. They are not always needed, especially if you know how to work around them.

For example, **My Computer** has a menu bar on it, yet the menu bar is hardly ever used, mainly because the same functions can be accomplished much quicker by clicking on the icons. Nevertheless, there are a lot of programs in Windows which do heavily depend upon the use of a menu bar and getting familiar with it is not a bad idea.

Most menu bars start with the word **File** and usually end with the word **Help**. As for the words in-between, they can vary somewhat. Below is a list of some of the most popular options found on a menu bar and what you can expect when you click on them:

File

This option is usually, if not always, listed first and for a good reason. Mainly because, it a good place to begin. In this option is where all the file decisions are made. This usually includes a collection of words; like **Open...**, **Save**, **Delete...**, **Print** or **Exit**. Basically, any kind of file manipulation can be done here.

Edit

This is commonly the second option in a menu bar. Sometimes, it isn't possible for certain windows, so it's occasionally left out. If a window has a Toolbar, then these options can also be found there. The Edit option is where all of the editing takes place. **Cutting**, **copying** and **pasting** are usually included within its selections, as well as some sort of **undo** command. Editing files is a lot like using paper, scissors and glue, only not as messy.

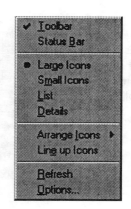

View

This option, like the Edit option, is not always available for certain windows. It is designed to allow users the ability to change the appearance of a particular window, mainly the contents within the window itself. For instance, if you can't see what is in a window, you can use this option to magnify it. The View option generally lets you choose between three to four different magnifications. They include: **Large icons**, **Small icons**, **List** and **Detail**. Each choice changes the appearance of the window's contents appropriately.

Options

This option usually provides, for lack of a better word, **options** which can be selected on a particular window. These options are very specific to the window they are attached to and do not apply towards any other windows. In addition, this is usually a good place to find **program preferences**.

Help

This option frequently accompanies every menu bar and is always located at the end. It basically provides two functions. The first one is fairly obvious. It offers **help!** Any time you have a question about a window or any of its contents, simply click on this option and an on-line assistance program will start. The second function of the Help option is to render **copyright information**. As boring as it may sound, this information has to be included with every Windows program.

What are Properties?

Properties mainly reveal information about a file; like where it is located or how much space it uses. Almost every icon or file in Windows has some sort of properties. They allow us to work with the object, without making any real changes to the data itself. The properties in a given object are more useful for "*informational*" purposes, than "*functional*" purposes.

For example, let's look at the properties of the card game **Solitaire**. Let's use it as a ginny pig. To see its properties click on its icon with the right-hand button and select the **Properties** option. (*Solitaire is usually located within the Taskbar menu, however for this example, we need to make a Shortcut for the game, in order to see its properties.*)

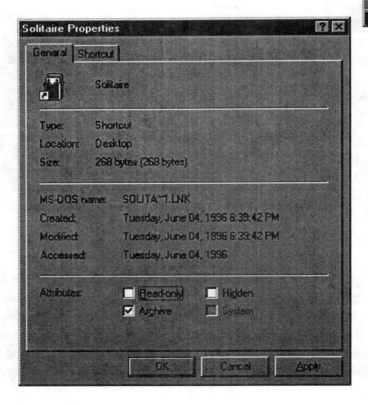

Figure 3.6
The Properties window for the card game of Solitaire

The Properties window for Solitaire, shown on the previous page is purely for informational purposes, with the exception of changing some of its attributes. The most important information is located at the top, starting with the **type** of file it is, its **location**, its **size** and its **contents**. This kind of information can be important when you are trying to locate file, rename it or delete it.

In earlier versions of Windows, the **P**r**operties** option provided the user with a greater amount of information, concentrating heavier on the locations and appearance of the files, rather than their size and characteristics.

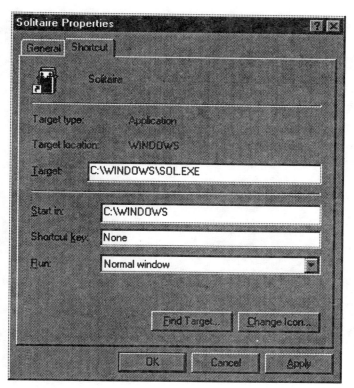

Figure 3.7
The Shortcut Information in the Properties window

More information can be obtained by looking at the **Shortcut** division of the Properties window. In the window shown above, you are allowed to change the icon associated with the file, as well as its shortcut. Shortcuts are new improvement to Windows, designed to make starting programs simpler and faster. They are covered in greater detail in the next chapter.

The Windows 95 Road Map

The Taskbar

Chapter 4

We are now ready to take a closer look at Windows 95. The first item you ought to recognize is a shiny rectangle which fills the bottom of the screen. It will customarily display the time at one end and the word **Start** at the other. This simple bar is one of the major distinctions between Windows 95 and its earlier versions. This rectangle is commonly known as the **Taskbar**. The Taskbar is the principal ingredient which helps give Windows 95 its new look.

44   Chapter Four

Figure 4.1
Windows 95 with the Taskbar

The Taskbar is a new Windows 95 term and much like former Windows terminology you won't find its definition in the dictionary. These words are unique to the world of computers and the sooner you introduce them into your vocabulary the better.

The Taskbar was designed to take over the responsibilities of the **Program Manager**. In early versions of Windows, the Program Manager was the primary link between the computer and its user. Today, even though the Taskbar's appearance is quite different from that of the Program Manager, they both basically provide the same service.

The Taskbar has a lot of advantages, when compared to the Program Manager of the past. It allows users to maneuver through windows much quicker than the conventional Program Manager and is a lot easier to use. Microsoft wanted to make running programs in Windows 95 faster and easier. The Taskbar cuts down time on searching for files and speeds up time on executing them. New and old Windows users should find the Taskbar extremely effortless and easy to pick up. In addition, the Taskbar does an excellent job at keeping the desktop interface clear and free of excess windows.

How to use the Taskbar

Initially, Windows 95 may seem to lack some of the flare seen in past versions, such as flashy interfaces combined with excessive clutter. Some users may have expected something a little more grand when they heard Microsoft was updating Windows 3.1. But, don't let its appearance fool you. The Taskbar will prove to be a great asset after you learn how to use it.

For starters, the size or thickness of the Taskbar is adjustable. Simply use the mouse to re-size it, much like the way you re-size windows. This way you can see more of what it is holding.

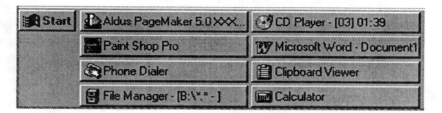

Figure 4.2
Adjusting the thickness of the Taskbar

You can make the Taskbar very large or you can re-size it so nothing shows up on the screen at all. In either case, the extremes tend to be a little overwhelming and not very useful.

You can also change the position of the Taskbar. Its default location is at the bottom of the screen, but it can be placed anywhere on the screen. It can moved to the sides or the top of the screen, if necessary. To move the Taskbar, simply use your mouse to grab it and move it in the direction you want. Subsequently, I think you will find the best place to house the Taskbar is at the bottom of the screen.

Another advantage of the Taskbar is, it's always present and easy to access. You will notice you cannot minimize or hide the Taskbar like you could with the Program Manager. Microsoft has made the Taskbar always visible, so it can always be accessed. The Taskbar works nicely with other programs, as well. Even when you are running them, the Taskbar makes room for itself wherever it can.

In the Taskbar, the space between the Start button and the clock, you'll find a series of buttons (or nametags) representing all the programs currently running at that time. Each of these buttons lets you access whatever program is printed on it. This is a helpful feature, because it makes switching between applications a breeze. To switch among them, simply click on the button of the program you wish to see. This way, there is no need to close or re-size windows to find other programs.

One of the main goals of the Taskbar is to organize all the running programs and then allow you to switch among them by clicking on the one you want. But, what about programs that are not currently running? A program will only show up on the Taskbar after it has been started.

In the case of starting a new program, there is only one way to do it. You have to use the **Start** button. The Start button does exactly what you would think; it starts things. You can even use the Start button to switch to a program that is already on the Taskbar.

Another popular way of switching from application to application is by using the "Alt + Tab" keys. To do this, hold down the Alt key and click on the Tab key. This will switch from program to program. While doing this, a little dialog box pops up and shows you which program is next.

The Start Button

The Start Button is basically a super-efficient program launcher. With this button, programs are easier and quicker to find and then start. There is no need to search through any more windows just to find a program. With Windows 95, simply click on the Start button and follow your intuition.

Another advantage of the Start button is it only takes <u>one</u> click to start a program, instead of a double-click. This way, you don't need a twitchy finger to start a program.

The Start button is used to initiate the **Start menu**. This menu was designed by Microsoft to include the most practical and useful options for its typical users. They wanted to avoid using technical words and keep the layout as uncomplicated as possible. The Start menu basically contains everything needed to fully utilize Windows 95. The list below gives a brief description of each option, while the rest of this chapter takes a closer look at each individual selection.

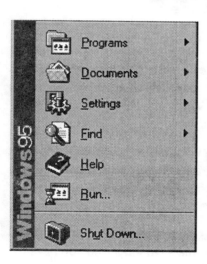

Programs: This option allows the user to quickly start (and find) any program in Windows 95.

Documents: This option allows the user to access the last 15 most recently opened documents.

Settings: This option allows the user to customize (or change) the settings of their system.

Find: This option helps users locate files.

Help: This option launches the Windows 95 Help program, which provides excellent on-screen assistance.

Run: This option is used to execute programs manually.

Shu**t down**: This option allows users to safely turn-off their computer and/or exit Windows 95.

48 Chapter Four

Programs

The **Programs** section of the Start menu will no doubt be one of the most active locations for many users. It allows them access to any of the executable programs on their computer. By using the mouse to navigate through a maze of nametags, users can easily find and start any program. The entire setup is designed to provide a path which leads its users directly to a program. Unlike earlier versions, where no sense of direction was ever present.

Figure 4.3
The Programs Section

Some of the nametags have triangles after their names. This means when clicked on, they open up a directory of programs, instead of starting one itself, as pointed out above. Similar to earlier versions of Windows, programs are sometimes kept in directories and to access them you must open the directory first.

Now, once you have found the program you want to run, all you need to do is click on it (once). After a few seconds, the program will start. In addition, you will notice a copy of the program's name placed in the Taskbar. This way you will always be able to find it.

At this point, the main focus of the Programs section should become clear; its usability. Everything in it is laid out like a explicit map. No longer do you have to search in vain through endless windows just to find a program.

Now, if you want to continue work on a project you may have started a while ago, you might want to look in the **Documents** section first. The Documents section has a collection of shortcuts. However, these shortcuts are not connected to programs, but instead they are connected directly to files the programs use. This way, Microsoft, in a manner of speaking, has set up a way to retrace your steps.

Documents

The **Documents** section is reserved for the 15 most recently opened documents. This means you will find a list of nametags which represent past and present documents. These nametags can then be clicked on to re-access the document without having to restart the program that originally created them first. Generally, these nametags are considered to be shortcuts.

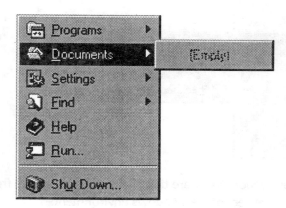

Figure 4.4
The Documents Section

As you work with the Document section, you could notice different things creeping into this section that may not seem like documents. This is because Windows defines documents unlike many users do. We may think of them as term papers, resumes or other lengthy official letters. But, for Windows, almost anything is a document. This includes wallpaper, sound & video clips, pictures, programs, presentations, faxes, text files or almost any other file from a Windows application. However, Windows 95 may not recognize all document formats, so some foreign documents may escape this section.

In addition, there is a **Clear** button in the Taskbar properties window which is designed to empty the contents of the Documents section. You will want to double check to make sure everything has been saved before clearing out this section.

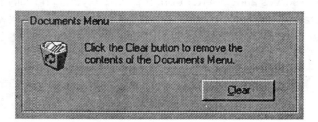

Figure 4.5
The **Clear** button in the Taskbar Properties window

Settings

The **Settings** option in the Start Menu contains a set of programs which help control the environment in Windows 95. Everything from the background colors to the speed of the mouse cursor is determined from within this section.

Figure 4.6
The Settings Option

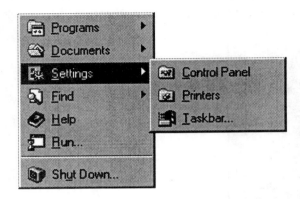

Within the Settings section, there are three selections to choose from. Each one controls a particular aspect of the Windows environment.

① The **Control Panel**: This controls general options for the entire system, including components like the display, keyboard, mouse and modems.

② The **Printers**: This controls general options for all printers, by helping them manage the job distribution and controlling the data flow. Since printers are a common component of many computers, much like a modem or keyboard, the preferences for them can also be found within the Control Panel.

③ The **Taskbar**: This controls the general options for the Taskbar, which act as the main interface between the user and Windows.

I will devote a complete chapter to the Control Panel, because it is a major part of Windows and deserves a lot of attention. It is where you can really manipulate a system's appearance and performance. It is a fun place to try out new ideas, and I will take a closer look at it in **Chapter 7**. Though, for right now, just be aware of its location.

Working with **Printers**

The second selection in the Settings is called **Printers**. This program basically manages all the printers on a system. If you do not have a printer, that is alright. Windows 95 is smart enough to check and see if a printer is actually attached.

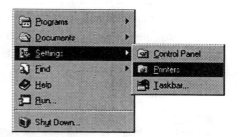

Now, if you do own a printer, it is here where you will find all of its set-up information. After clicking on this option, the **Printers window** will appear. It should look something like the window shown below, depending greatly on kinds of printers you own.

Figure 4.7
The Printers window

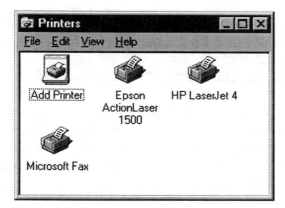

The Printers window may look a little strange at first. It could seem a bit confusing and difficult to understand what exactly is being displayed. To a novice user, the printers in this window may be easily confused with actual printers. However, these are not real printers at all, they are printer **drivers**.

What is a driver? A driver is a piece of software which connects external devices to Windows; like keybaords, monitors, or in this case, a printer.

So, why are there so many printer drivers? In Windows, some printers can use more than one driver. Different drivers work better than others. Some printer drivers are made for particular jobs, like the Microsoft Fax driver. It functions as a fax machine for Windows. Therefore the number of drivers to not aways have to correspond with the number of real printers.

Once a driver is double-clicked, it becomes the **default** driver for the computer. Therefore, you can decide which printer driver you want to use simply by double-clicking on it. You can also change its settings here or in the applications themselves, like WordPerfect, Lotus 1-2-3 or any other popular program. In addition, after double-clicking on a driver, you are allowed to intervene with the printing process.

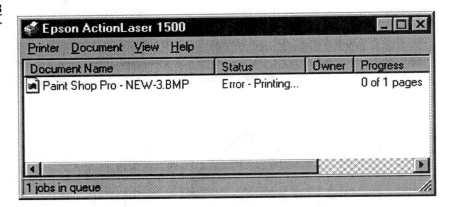

Figure 4.8
The Printer Driver dialog box

As you can see the window shown above looks pretty empty. This is because most of the time it will contain nothing, after all I am usually not printing. However, with the window shown above, you can see the name of one document in the dialog box and its status. Here you have the option of **stopping** or **pausing** this job if you want to. Subsequently, this is a good place to look if you are encountering problems when printing.

After examining the Printers window, you will probably notice most of the options in its menu bar are essentially useless. The **File** option allows you to pause and set the default printers, basically the same things you could have done after clicking on that printer's icon. The **Edit** option is quite unusable in most situations and the **View** option only changes the display of the icons.

Most issues dealing with printing occur behind closed doors. What this means, is the computer does most of the printing automatically and if any problems occur, it will tell you while the job is being sent to the printer. As long as the printer preferences have been set up right, the problems which take place will have more to do with your printer than with any of its drivers, like the printer running out of paper.

Setting up the Taskbar

The last selection in the **Settings** is the **Taskbar**. Sure enough, you probably thought you had heard the last of the Taskbar at the beginning of this chapter. Well, you only got half the story. You already know what the Taskbar is. This section is where you can customize it.

Unfortunately, there isn't much you can do with the appearance of the Taskbar itself. It will always be a rectangle somewhere on the screen, though you can customize it a little. Start by clicking on **Settings** and then on **Taskbar**, after which, a new window should emerge, as shown below.

Figure 4.9
The Taskbar Properties window

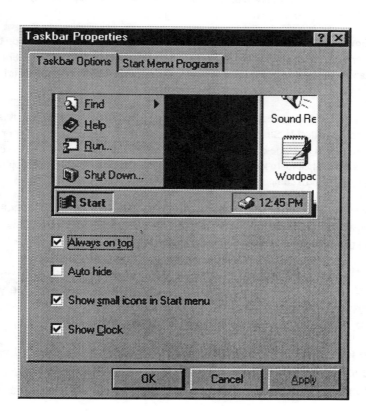

The Taskbar Properties window is divided into two parts; **Taskbar Options** and **Start Menu Programs**. Both parts deal exclusively with the Start menu and the Taskbar, mainly concentrating on the Programs section.

In the **Taskbar Options** window, you have the opportunity to customize the Taskbar itself. Unfortunately, you are not allowed to do much changing. Microsoft has made the Taskbar as a steady point of reference and did not want it to be altered too much in any way. So, there are only four parts of the Taskbar which can be modified. Here is a list of what you can change.

① **Always on top**, you can decide if you want the Taskbar always visible. It is a good idea to have the Taskbar present at all times, since it proves to be a handy tool and does not take up much screen space.

② **Auto hide**, you can automatically hide the Taskbar from the users view. This does not mean the Taskbar will be hidden permanently, this option only allows objects to cover its face only temporarily. I recommend leaving this option off.

③ **Show small icons in Start menu**, you can change the display of the boxes on the Start menu. So instead of having large boxes of programs which take up the entire screen, you can shrink the size of those icons down a little. Either way, the difference is hardly worth showing.

④ **Show Clock**, you guessed it. If you do or don't want to know what time it is, this is where you decide. Simply check the box if you want a clock on the Taskbar or uncheck it if you aren't in a time-crunching mood. Personally, I suggest you leaving the clock on, since it is always helpful to keep an eye on the clock since time has a way of slipping by when you are using a computer.

As you decide to alter the Taskbar, you'll notice the little picture included within the window updates to show you how the new changes will look. This way, you can judge the outcome before actually completing the change.

The last part of the Taskbar Properties window is called the **Start Menu Programs** and to fully understand the connection it has with the Taskbar, you must first comprehend what it does.

Its job is to organize all the software within the Start menu, in particular, in the **Programs** section. It is here where old and new programs are added to and removed from the Start menu. Since all programs have to be introduced to the system somewhere, it makes sense to have the Taskbar be one of the first objects they meet.

The Taskbar

To examine this section, start by clicking on Start Menu Programs. This will cause a new window to appear. This window doesn't give you much freedom. You really only have three alternatives.

① **Add...** Adds to new program (or title) to the Start menu.
② **Remove...** Removes an existing program (or title) from the Start menu.
③ **Advanced...** Moves programs around the Start menu.

Remember, the Taskbar is only an interface for Windows. It represents a link to each program, not the programs themselves. So, when programs are added to or removed from the Taskbar, only the interface of these programs are affected and not the programs themselves.

For example, if you decide to move a program into the Accessories directory, you are only moving the link of that program. All the files would remain in the same location as when they were first installed. To move files themselves, you would want to use the Windows Explorer or My Computer.

Likewise, deleting files from the Start menu does not necessary mean you are removing them from the entire system. It only means you are making these files more difficult to find, by destroying their link to Windows.

Figure 4.10
Start Menu Programs window

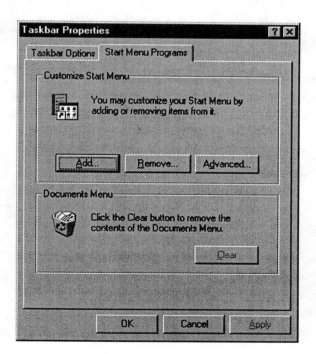

Finding Files

Windows 95 has a nice program which helps you find just about anything. It is far more advanced than past searching programs and is one of the highlights of this new operating system. Here is how it works.

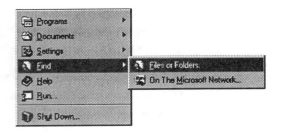

Click on the **Find** option in the **Start menu**. Then type in your best recollection of the file name. After a few seconds, you should see the file you are looking for.

Figure 4.11
The Find dialog box

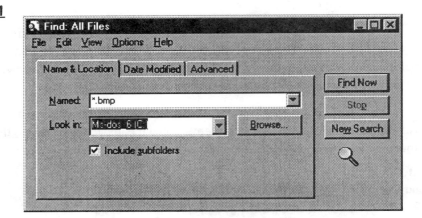

If you are having problems remembering the file's name, you can also search by last modification date, size of the file or even text within a document. With all of these features, you'll find it very difficult to lose anything in Windows.

Figure 4.12
Finding lost Files

Help!

Windows 95 has an excellent Help program built in. It provides you with instant on-line help, where no area has been left out. You can either search through the Help program using its table of contents or, if you get stuck on a particular problem just press the "**F1**" key.

The Help program in Windows 95 is designed to replace the more traditional method of assistance which common came in the form of user manuals. This program is presented in a very readable fashion and goes far beyond the limits of user friendliness. However, it does still require a large degree of effort and understanding. After all, if you are having problems with Windows, using a Windows program to help you is like getting assistance from the problem-maker itself.

Aside from the Help program in Windows 95, there are also computer books like mine available. Computer books offer much more than their software equivalent. They provide great examples as well as unrivaled human experiences. In addition, they are also very portable and even work when a computer is turned off.

Figure 4.13
The Help Program

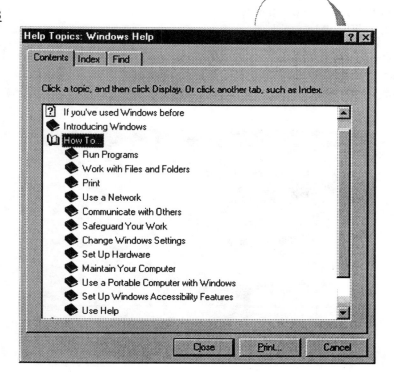

Run and Shut Down

At the base of the Start menu there are two final options. They are the **Run...** and **Shutdown...** buttons and both have exactly opposite jobs.

Figure 4.14
The Run dialog box

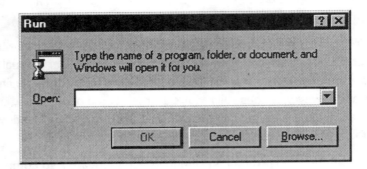

The **Run...** button allows a user to run any program, manually, by typing in the executable command at the Run window. This was designed to be a no nonsense way of executing a program, which stems from the earliest days of Windows. Though the Run... button is seldom used, the Shutdown... button, on the other hand, is difficult to avoid.

The **Shutdown...** button is new to Windows. Before, Windows had to trick its users into closing applications in order to safely shut-down the system. With Windows 95, this task is candy-coated with a button and some simple instructions.

Figure 4.15
Turning off a computer

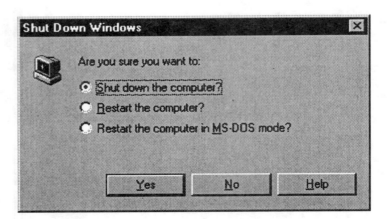

My Computer and the Windows Explorer

CHAPTER 5

The Windows Explorer and My Computer are very similar programs, although they are both located in different places. The Explorer is located with all the other system programs, while My Computer is located at the top of the start up screen. Both programs allow users to access and manipulate files on their computers. However, the main difference between the two is; the Explorer concentrates mainly on internal files, where as My Computer tends to focus on the entire system.

My Computer

My Computer, it sounds like a real predicable title for a computer book. It's short and to the point. It leaves little room for guessing and presents itself in a manner a child could understand. Well, as innocent as it sounds, Microsoft picked this name to represent a part of Windows 95. The part which plays true to its name. Simply put, My Computer is Windows' way of describing your computer.

My Computer is a small icon, commonly found in the left hand corner of the screen. It presents a picture of a small computer and invites you to click on it. The urge to do so, will open up a new door to examine the computer in a way you have never seen. For the first time you will have a chance to experience your entire system, not as the way humans do, but as the way Windows does.

My Computer is one of the first places new users should examine. It provides them with all the fundamentals of their system. In general, the information it displays should not be considered a mystery, since most users should already be away of their computer's specifications. However, if any reassurances are necessary, then this is the place to look.

Figure 5.1
My Computer

My Computer

My Computer takes one approach at describing a computer. At first, it displays all the drives within a system, these include **disk drives** and **hard drives**. Some examples of disk drives are CD-ROM drives, back-up tape drives or floppy disk drives. These are usually found in the front of a computer and are pretty easy to locate.

My Computer and The Windows Explorer

As for hard drives, they are not as visible. Hard drives are permanently placed inside a computer. They are like a huge parking garage. They store massive amounts of data; usually in the form of documents, programs or files.

A hard drive can hold a lot more data than a diskette can. So, it makes good sense to stock-pile all the large programs there, like Windows 95. Everyone has at least one hard drive. This drive is commonly known as the **C** drive and it is considered home for most programs and files. However, it is possible to have more than one hard drive. If you owned a second hard drive, it would be called a **D** drive. And if you had a network of drives, they would be labeled all the way up to **Z**.

My Computer basically provides a "*table of contents*" of a computer, which starts on the **C** drive. From there you are given a map to the entire computer.

Figure 5.2
Working around My Computer

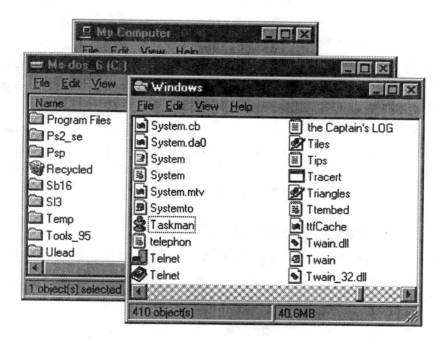

My Computer not only allow users to access files, but manipulate them as well. Users can move, rename and delete files. These type of actions are very important and very powerful as well.

Chapter Five

Moving files around My Computer

Organization is very important in computers. It helps improve their speed and can preserve valuable drive space. In addition, an organized computer is much easier to work on, since it helps when you do not have to search for files or programs.

Moving files around in Windows is one way of keeping organized. This can be done within My Computer, as well as other programs, like the Windows Explorer. Moving a file in My Computer involves physically dragging the icons around the screen; although sometimes it may seem unclear where these files are going?

Microsoft has tried to eliminate some of this confusion by making a icon or file change color when it is dragged. Also, if you move it to the correct place, a plus (+) sign will appear, otherwise you'll see an out-of-bounds sign. Now, if you are ready to do some arranging, follow these steps:

❶ To move a file, start with double-clicking on the **C** drive within My Computer. After a few seconds, a window will appear displaying the contents of the hard drive.

❷ The next step is to click on the file you want to move. It should become highlighted. Using the mouse, pick up the file and drop it in the location you want it to go. It is that simple. You don't even have to type anything, everything is automatically updated by Windows.

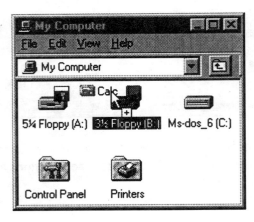

Figure 5.3
Moving a File

The best kind of file handling you can do in My Computer is with the files themselves. This means doing operations like deleting or renaming the files. Although, you want to be very careful when you do this type of file manipulation. Because renaming a file is an easy way of losing it, and deleting a file is a good way of destroying it!

Renaming files

Why would anyone want to rename a file? There are a lot of good reasons for renaming files. First, you may not like the name of a particular program, or you may want to use a more descriptive title. Whatever the reason, renaming files is very common in Windows and sometimes can't be avoided.

One way of renaming files is by using My Computer. Simply locate the file you want to rename and click on it. This will cause the selected file to become highlighted. Then click the **File** option from the menu bar and choose **Rename**. At this point, the only thing left to do is to think of a name. You can also use the F2 key to manually rename files.

Figure 5.4
Renaming a File

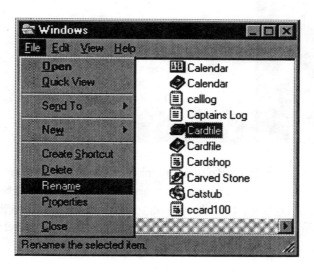

Remember when renaming files, you are making permanent changes. Therefore, I recommend not renaming any important file. Because some programs may use these files. If you change their name, these programs won't be able to find the right file! So before you do decide to rename a file, make sure you know what it does and choose an appropriate name you won't forget.

Deleting files

Deleting a file is very similar to renaming it. Only instead of changing the name of the file, with deleting, you change the file itself. To delete a file, follow the same steps as renaming a file, only choose the **Delete** option instead of rename.

Please keep in mind, once a file is deleted, it is gone. So pay close attention to the files you delete. In most cases, try not to delete files. Instead of deleting them, try renaming them first. Then test your system to see if there is any damage. Another suggestion is to try moving a file into a temporary place before deleting it. Then test your system to see if there is any damage. With these methods, you can always get the file back.

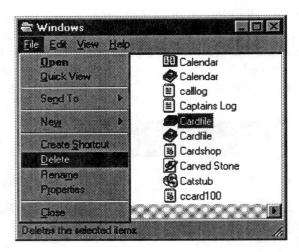

Figure 5.5
Deleting a File

But, if you do happen to delete a file by mistake, you are not completely out of luck. Microsoft has designed a new program in Windows 95 which holds on to deleted files for a short time. This allows you to retrieve them before they vanish into binary heaven. It is called the **Recycle Bin**, and I will discuss how to use it in the next chapter.

Making Shortcuts

Another way of accessing files is by using **Shortcuts**. What is a Shortcut? A Shortcut, like the name implies, allows users to start a program, without having to find it first. As if finding programs in Windows 95 wasn't easy enough, with Shortcuts, users can create a button to start any program. This button is placed on the desktop and can be used anytime. Subsequently, these time savers are made within My Computer.

You can make a Shortcut for any program or file on the computer. They are best applied towards programs which you use all the time. Let's say you happen play Solitaire a lot. You could get tired of going through the chore of finding it every time you want to play. Well, with Windows 95, you can create a Shortcut for Solitaire. Here is how to do it:

❶ Start with locating the Solitaire icon in My Computer. You should find it on the **C** drive within the **Windows** directory. Once you have found it, click on it, so it becomes highlighted.

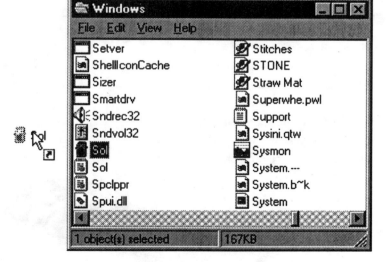

Figure 5.6
Locating and Dragging, to make a Shortcut

❷ Using the mouse, drag the Solitaire icon out of the window and place it on the desktop.

❸ When finished, remember to close all the windows you just opened.

Deleting Shortcuts

To get delete a Shortcut is very simple and takes a couple of seconds. Start by highlighting the icon of the Shortcut you want to delete. Then just click the **right-hand** mouse button and a drop down menu will appear. Choose the **Delete** option, and the Shortcut will disappear.

Figure 5.7
Deleting a Shortcut

Keep in mind, when deleting a Shortcut, you are <u>not</u> destroying the actual program, only its Shortcut (icon) is destroyed. Now, with a little practice, you will be able to set up your computer to fit your daily needs. By making Shortcuts, you will help organize your system and make it more efficient.

The Windows Explorer

The Windows Explorer is a lot like My Computer. However, it has even more in common with the **File Manager** from Windows 3.1. They both have comparable layouts which provide similar information.

The File Manager was one of the main programs in Windows 3.1, which was responsible for regulating files. It was one of the only ways to directly access a file and served a universal role as the main door to a computer.

The Explorer performs these roles as well, but it is suited more towards a Windows 95 audience. Here are some other key distinctions:

① The Explorer allows long file names, unlike the File Manager, which would only recognize the first eight characters of a file.

② The Explorer allows users to access, not only files, but icons as well. For example, My Computer is present in the Explorer, even though it is represented on the desktop as an icon, rather than a file. Accessing icons in the File Manager was not possible (granted Windows 3.1 did not have a lot of extra icons either).

③ With the Explorer, it is possible to access locations in Windows, which otherwise would be impossible. For example, you can look inside of the Control Panel or the Recycler. This was not possible in the File Manager.

For previous Windows 3.1 users, the Explorer should be instinctively easy to understand. As for the rest of you, I am sure you will find using the Explorer to be worthwhile and relatively painless.

Like any program, the Windows Explorer has a purpose or a job. It's main duty can be summed up in the war expression, seek out and destroy. After all, it's the Explorer's job to oversee all the files in the computer and allow you access to them. Once you have access to them, you can manipulate these files much like you could in My Computer. This includes moving files, renaming files and deleting files. In addition, the Explorer allows you to also make Shortcuts. These Shortcuts are made in the exact same manner as they were with My Computer.

Moving files in the Windows Explorer

Let's say you want to move a file into the Windows directory, a picture for example. With the Windows Explorer, such a task is quite simple and only takes a few seconds. Not only that, moving files within the Explorer can be done without using the keypad. Here's how:

❶ Start with locating the file you want to move.

Figure 5.8
Locating a File using the Explorer

In the screen shown above, you should notice the further you move towards the right, the deeper you plunge into the computer. What this means is, you will always find the files on the **right** and where they came from on the **left**.

The left side will always be composed of indexes, everything from drives to directories. Each file on a computer has an index which goes with it, these indexes are called **paths** and they make up the location for any given file. Paths are important because without them, a computer couldn't locate anything. In fact, when you delete a file, it is the path which is destroyed, not the actual file, it remains untouched.

My Computer and The Windows Explorer

❷ Once you have located a file, it can be moved, simply by picking the file up and dragging it to the correct location. As the moving file nears its target, each location will light up. Just drop the file in the correct location as you pass it.

Figure 5.9
Moving a file using the Windows Explorer

When the file is dropped into its new location, its old location will no longer exist. This is because the file was actually **moved**, not copied. It is important to note, when you drag files among folders (on the same drive), they are <u>moved</u>. However, if you drag a file to another drive, then it is <u>copied</u>. Now, if you want to copy (not move) files among folders on the same drive, just follow the same steps as above, but hold down the **"Ctrl"** key during the dragging process.

> A **folder** is Windows' way of saying a directory. It is actually a simple graphical representation of a directory.

The Windows Explorer was designed to do exactly what its name implies, explore. If you have ever felt the desire to check out your system, this is the tool to use. It is powerful, compact and complete with all the options you will need to manipulate any files and their locations.

However, it is very likely when probing your system, you will come across files which you may not understand or could appear foreign to you, almost as if they belong on another planet. How ever strong the urge may be to clean them up, I strongly recommend leaving these files alone.

The Recycle Bin

CHAPTER 6

It seems everyone is recycling these days, including Microsoft. Though their contribution won't save any trees, it might save you a lot of time and heartache. Microsoft has incorporated into Windows 95 a built-in recycler, and it works like this. When you delete a file, a copy of that file is automatically put into a special part of memory called the **Recycle Bin**. Then, if you discover deleting this file was a mistake, you can easily retrieve it from the Recycle Bin without any hassles. The Recycle Bin has been a long awaited improvement to Windows.

How to use the Recycle Bin

The Recycle Bin can be instantly found when you start up Windows 95. It is represented by an icon revealing a small wastebasket with green circular arrows on it. It customarily resides in the top left hand corner of the screen, just below the My Computer icon. It is always available and constantly waiting to be used. The recycler makes deleting files from Windows 95 safe and easy.

There are many different ways of using the Recycle Bin, here is one way; first, start with finding it some food.

❶ Choose a program or file you want to delete.

❷ Grab it and drag it into the Recycle Bin.

Even though, the file was physically put in the Recycle Bin, the same effect could have been achieved by a more conventional method. Mainly because, every time you delete a file, knowingly or not, a copy of that file is placed into the Recycle Bin.

Unfortunately, this only holds true with Windows 95 programs. The Recycle Bin is not compatible and does not work with the old File Manager or any DOS programs.

Now, once a file is in the Recycle Bin, it is either kept until needed again or if preferred, completely disposed of. This way, the Recycle Bin becomes a waiting station for files.

But how long will the Recycle Bin hold on to these files? That depends heavily on drive space. Because most people delete files to gain or optimize hard drive space, the recycler itself has to keep a close eye on its contents; since it too takes up hard disk space. A full Recycle Bin can consume 10 percent of a hard drive. Now, once it reaches 10 percent, the recycler begins to purge the oldest files in it first, to achieve the utmost space efficiency.

If having the recycler eliminate files automatically bothers you, then don't worry. You can control how long the recycler holds all the deleted files. This is done by changing the percentage of disk space it is allowed to occupy. To see this click on the Recycle Bin using the right mouse button, then choose the **P**r**operties...** option from the drop down menu, as shown below.

Figure 6.1
The Properties option

This open the Recycle Bin Properties window. This window allows us to customize the recycler quite drastically. In the Recycle Bin Properties window, you can even eliminate the option of a recycler altogether. But, more frequently, this window is used to provide an opportunity to adjust the percentage of drive space the Recycle Bin is permitted to use. By adjusting this percentage, you can extend or shorten the list of the residents in the Recycle Bin, thereby controlling their life-span. If you want the recycler to hang on to more deleted files, just increase the percentage. Otherwise, if you want the deleted files to have a shorter trip to computer heaven, simply decrease the percentage. Either way, you are in complete control of all the deleted file's destiny. The Recycle Bin Properties window is shown on the next page.

Figure 6.2
The Recycle Bin Properties window

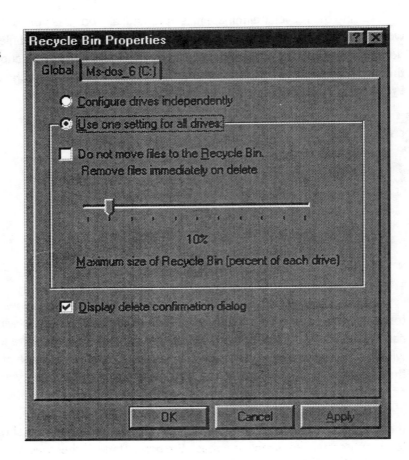

As you can see, the options in the Recycle Bin Properties window are pretty powerful and can be easily abused if not used correctly. Let me describe these options a little more.

- ☑ The first check-box, allows you to bypass the recycler entirely. I would strongly recommend leaving this option alone, unless you are fairly confident and have plenty of disk space. The other options are less consequential, although equally as important.

- ☑ The bottom check-box basically has the system confirm exactly what it is deleting. This is a good idea, because it is very often in this high-tech world we find ourselves deleting files, when we have no idea of what they do. This option just helps to document it.

Working with the Recycle Bin

Since working around Windows 95 is so easy, sometimes making a mistake can be easy, too. In these cases, the Recycle Bin can prove to be a very good friend once you learn how to use it. It can really save a lot of time and some day, it may actually save your behind!

The Recycle Bin preserves many different kinds of file formats. It can hold documents, drawings, sounds, icons, shortcuts, video clips, e-mail, faxes, pictures and even some small programs.

Once a file is in the Recycle Bin, it can be restored back to its original location, if necessary, at any time. However, as long as it remains in the recycler, a file is considered to be unusable by the computer. This is until the file is retrieved. To retrieve a file from the Recycle Bin, start with double-clicking on the Recycle Bin icon, this will open a window similiar to the one shown below.

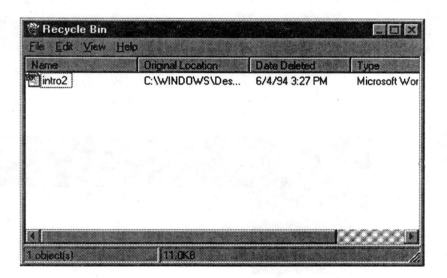

Figure 6.3
The Recycle Bin window

Obviously, the window shown above is revealing. A sigh of relief should be exhaled after its appearance. As you can see, it clearly displays all the deleted files along with their original location, the day they were deleted and what type of file they were. At the bottom of the window, you can see just how much space each deleted file occupied. If this information is not present, select **Details** from the **View** pull-down menu, as shown on the next page.

Figure 6.4
The View Option in the Recycle Bin

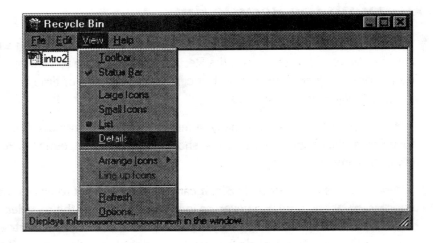

The Recycle Bin was designed for new users in particular. It helps alleviate some of the stress involved with managing files on a computer. It leaves plenty of room for careless errors and the minor accidents which often accompany novice users. Basically, it gives users a second chance.

Once a file has gone in the Recycle Bin, there are only two ways to get it out. Either a file is retrieved or it is demolished. Both alternatives are executed in similar fashions. Start with selecting **File** from the menu bar, as shown below.

Figure 6.5
Working with the Recycle Bin

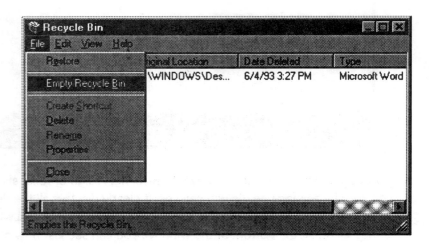

Most of the options in the **F**ile pull-down menu are only available after a file has been highlighted (or selected). Once highlighted, a varity of actions can be performed on the file, to decide its fate. Here is a list of those actions and their outcomes.

R**e**store

This will restore the highlighted file to its original location. This is essentially the main purpose of the Recycler. If you do not have a particular file highlighted, the **R**e**store** option will not be available.

Empty Recycle **B**in

This empties or deletes the entire contents of the Recycle Bin. Highlighted or not, clicking on this option destroys all the files in the Recycle Bin. After selecting this option, you are given one final opportunity to change your mind. By this point, you had better know what you are deleting!

Figure 6.6
A Files Last Words

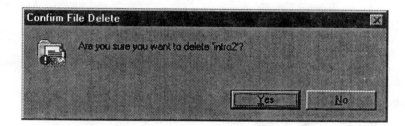

Delete

This deletes only the highlighted files and if no files are highlighted, then this option will not be available. It is very similar to the **Empty Recycle B**in option, however it works only with selected files, instead of the entire Bin.

Properties...

This option gives you a closer look at the file which is highlighted. Here you can see all the secret information about the file. This is a good place to look before deleting a file. It tells you how the file was created, where it came from, the size of the file, its creation dates and its deletion dates. This window also includes some attributes about the file, as well.

Figure 6.7
The Properties window

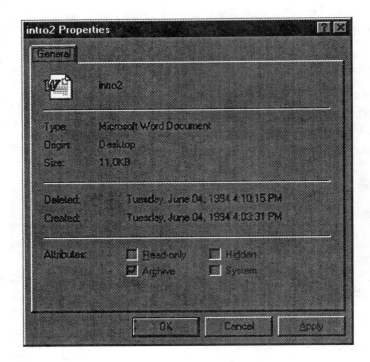

At this point, the role and limitations of the Recycle Bin should be clear. It is basically a safety net for computer users. And like a safety net, it will always be there. However, even safety nets sometimes break. Some files are critical for day-to-day processing and when they are deleted, the outcome could be very severe. In these extreme cases, even the Recycle Bin could shutdown.

The Control Panel

CHAPTER 7

The Control Panel is one program which previous Windows 3.1 users may find familiar. It was a standard part of all the earlier versions of Windows and continues to fulfill a useful function today. Although the contents of the Control Panel may look a little different, its general purpose still remains the same. It is used to provide a link between a computer and the Windows interface. It helps interpret each component of a computer so it is compatible with Windows. Even as components are upgraded, it is the Control Panel's job to make sure they continue to agree with the entire system.

The Control Panel

Don't let the Control Panel's name scare you! This program is easy to operate and can be very useful, not to mention fun. To find this program, click on **Settings** option in the Start menu and then select the **Control Panel**. Within seconds the Control Panel window will open up, as shown below.

Figure 7.1
The Control Panel

Each icon in the Control Panel represents a different component or part of a system. Since all computers contain different components, not everyone's Control Panel will look the same. In the diagram above, only the most common elements of today's computers are shown, but your Control Panel could easily show more or less. In this chapter, I will take a closer look at each one of these components.

Once in the Control Panel, to access a component you simply double click on its icon. Doing so will actually open the properties window for that icon. Property windows are found in many places, besides the Control Panel and are used to provide users with a full description of any component or file. These descriptions usually are quite technical in nature and can include information about file sizes, file types and their locations.

However, the property windows in the Control Panel are much more extensive and include greater amount of detail compared with any other ones. The properties in the Control Panel allow users to make physical changes, which in turn affects the entire system. This is what makes the Control Panel operate like a command center, putting you in the captain's chair.

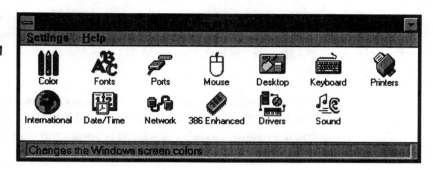

Figure 7.2
The Control Panel from Windows 3.1

For the rest of this chapter, I will take a closer look at each icon in the Control Panel, starting from the top and working my way down. You may have noticed some of these icons already occupy other chapters in this book. In those cases, I will just direct you to the correct chapter, instead of rewriting all the information again.

Keep in mind, merely being placed in the Control Panel is an honor for an icon. It means each icon is there for a reason, and despite first impressions, each icon has an important job. Therefore, any changes made in the Control Panel will have global effects as far as your system is concerned, so be careful.

Add New Hardware

Add New Hardware is the first icon in the Control Panel and subsequently is seldom ever used. It is designed to let users tell Windows (manually) about new hardware devices which have been installed. Many times Windows 95 will detect these changes first, so running this program is usually not necessary.

Subsequently, this is one of those topics which deserves an entire chapter and rightfully so, it has one. This topic is covered when I discuss Plug and Play in **Chapter 17**. Plug and Play is a new concept unique to Windows 95 and allows users to plug in devices and then proceed to use them (hence its name).

Add/Remove Programs

Add/Remove Programs is the second icon in the Control Panel and it allows users to install new programs on to their system. Even though this is not the only way to install programs, it is one of the easiest and most complete ways.

Nearly all software usually include some kind of installation files, commonly called **install.exe** or **setup.exe**. The only tricky part about using these files is finding them first. With Windows 95, you can use Add/Remove Programs to search the software's diskette for the installation file. This way, all the work is done for you by Windows.

There are many other ways of installing software. You can use the **Start** menu, **My Computer**, the **Windows Explorer** or even the **File Manager**. In any event, the main idea is to find the new software's installation program and start it (*install.exe* or *setup.exe*).

Another great advantage of using Add/Remove Programs is its ability to remove unwanted programs. This may seem a little foolish at first, but there is more to removing a program from Windows than one might think. For one reason, the Windows environment itself is so intertwined, that a single program may leave traces of itself in many different locations. So when a program is deleted, sometimes traces of that program remain.

In reality, this isn't a problem until disk space becomes essential, since all those traces of old programs take up disk space even if they are not being used. You can avoid problems like this by using **Add/Remove Programs** to remove all the unwanted programs from your computer.

Adding or removing software is quite simple in Windows 95. Start by double-clicking on the **Add/Remove Programs** icon in the **Control Panel**. This will open up a properties window, which contains a list of all the software previously installed by Windows. From this list you can choose what to get rid of or add to.

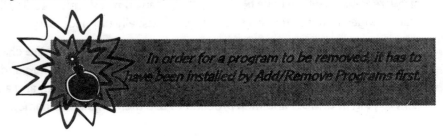

In order for a program to be removed, it has to have been installed by Add/Remove Programs first.

Figure 7.3
The Add/Remove Programs window

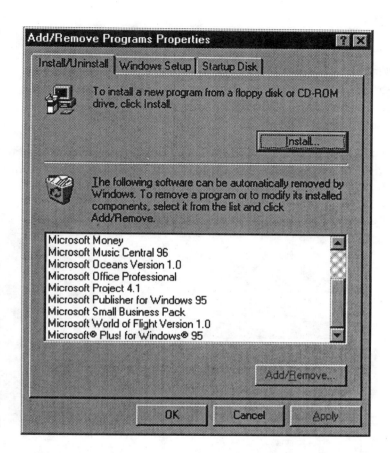

In the window shown above, all you need to decide whether to install a new program or remove an existing one.

- ✓ To install a new program, insert the first diskette into a disk drive (or the CD into a CD-ROM drive) and click on the **Install...** button.
- ✓ To remove an existing program, select the file you want to remove and click on the **Add/Remove...** button. By using this program, you can be assured all traces of that program will be removed.

Add/Remove Programs Properties window contains some other options, as well (*i.e. Windows setup and Startup Disk*). These options correspond to adding or removing extra files to the operating system itself; like additional sounds, screen savers, wallpaper or even games. Since Windows is such a large operating system, not all the files may have been fully installed during its initial installation.

Date/Time

The **Date/Time**, found in the Control Panel, is the main clock for Windows 95. It uses this clock to schedule events and track system usage. In addition, for the users who shut their machines down at night, this clock allows Windows to know where it is when it wakes up.

To get a better idea, click on the **Date/Time** icon in the Control Panel. It will open the Date/Time Properties window. Another way to open this window is to double-click on the time in the Taskbar.

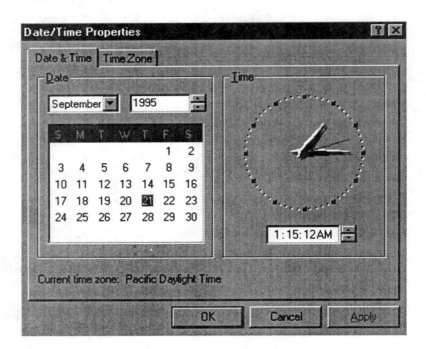

Figure 7.4 Date/Time Properties window

In the window shown above, you are allowed to adjust the day and time, if necessary. This is very useful during **Daylight Savings** time changes, as well as any time changes during lengthy travels. However, this is probably the only practical opportunity you will have to adjust the time. Since Windows derives its time from the system clock which works off an internal battery, power outages do not present any dilemma, unlike natural clocks or the ones on VCRs.

In addition, it is important to note, Windows time is not necessarily the same as System time. A computer has a system clock, where it derives its time from. Windows, on the other hand, derives its time from the window shown on the previous page. Originally, when Windows was first installed, it looked at the system clock to get the time. But after that, you are given the ability to change it. Subsequently, you do not have the ability to change the system clock, it is kind of like an odometer on a car.

Changing the time in this window only affects Windows and any of its applications. It does not have a significant effect on the age of the computer. Despite all the rumors you may have heard, this is not the fountain of youth for your system. However, since Windows 95 does control more of a computer than it ever has in the past, the ability to change this time is as close as you'll ever get to touching the system's youth.

Display

The **Display** icon is probably going be the most used part of the Control Panel. Therefore it deserves a separate chapter.
It basically controls what you see; everything from the wallpaper on the screen, to the colors of each window. It is also in charge of the screen savers. To read more about the Display, check out **Chapter 8**.

Fonts

What is a font? A font is a style of type, much like someone's own hand writing. There are many different kinds of fonts. In addition, new fonts are being produced everyday, so the limit of fonts is unimaginable. Some fonts are popular and very noticable. For instance, the font which Coca Cola uses is so distinctive, you can recognize their product even if you can't read the text.

The **Font folder**, in the Control Panel, helps organize all the system fonts. In order for a font to run on a computer, it has to be in this folder. In most cases, the list of fonts will be rather large, because Windows 95 itself automatically comes with around **71** fonts.

Figure 7.5
The Fonts window

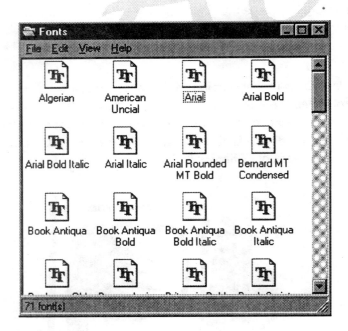

In the window shown above, you get a brief description of all the fonts. Each font includes a name and a picture. The picture, slightly above its name, tells you what kind of font it is. The "**TT**" stands for a **TrueType** font, where as an "**A**" stands for a **Printer** font.

In general, Printer fonts are not as clear as TrueType fonts and print rather jaggedly. Although, the difference may go unnoticed, it is always better to use a TrueType font.

If you are interested in any of the fonts and would like to see what they look like, double click on it. This will display a sample of that particular font. You can even print the sample if you want to. For instance, double clicking on the icon marked **Arial** will produce the sample shown below.

Figure 7.6
A Sample of a True-Type Font

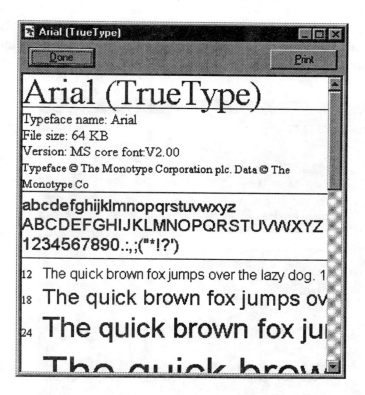

Additional Fonts can be loaded into a computer, as well. There is a lot of software available which only contain fonts, some containing thousands of them.

Installing additional fonts into the font folder is rather easy. Simply start by putting the diskette into a disk drive and then click on the **File** pull down menu. From there select **Install New Font...** and the rest is done automatically.

Fonts are not only used in Windows 95, but in other programs as well. Many word processors, desktop publishers and other business applications all use fonts to produce professional-looking documents. Since Windows 95 is an operating system, its fonts can be shared by any program running within its environment. This holds true for other programs, as well.

Internet

This icon is available to the users who have access to the Internet through Microsoft's Internet program, which is currently packaged with the **Plus**. Otherwise, it isn't really useful since most of the connections between the Internet and Windows are handled separately. However, if you do happen to use Microsoft's Internet program coupled with an access provider, then you can set up its connections in this window.

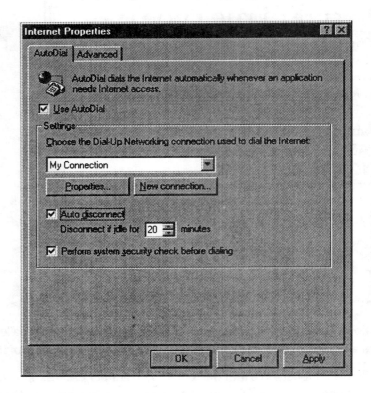

Figure 7.7
The Internet Properties window

Besides the Internet information, the rest of this window can get pretty technical. It mostly deals with networking and communication software issues. This window can also probe connections you made with HyperTerminal.

HyperTerminal is a new communication program included with Windows 95. It is an updated version of the older program which was a part of the Windows 3.1 package. HyperTerminal is discussed later on. Subsequently, you can learn about the Internet in **Chapters 16** and **20**.

Joystick

The **Joystick** icon is used to calibrate and test joysticks for Windows. Though, keep in mind that most games will want to calibrate joysticks separately, so calibrating it with Windows doesn't always amount to much.

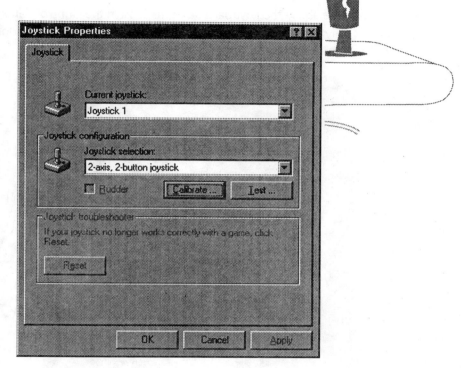

Figure 7.8
The Joystick Properties window

What exactly does calibrate mean? When calibrating a joystick, you are defining its limits so it does not over-run the screen. This allows different manufactures to make a wide range of joysticks which are compatible with the same game. Calibration also sets up the joystick so it will not conflict with Windows or any other programs.

After calibrating it, you will want to test the joystick to make sure the it works correctly. This is done by clicking on the **Test...** button.

If by chance your joystick won't work, you may want to double check its connections and then try re-installing the software included with it. I know from experience, Windows 95 can be pretty picky when it comes to joysticks.

Keyboard

The **Keyboard** plays an obvious role in any computer's daily routine. It acts as the major input device and seldom receives any help, with the exception of an occasion click from a mouse.

Despite the abuse the keyboard takes, its icon in the Control Panel is rarely used. It is only useful in making speed or language adjustments and does not allow users to do much else.

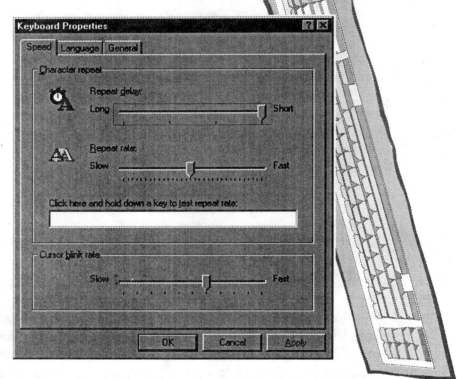

Figure 7.9
The Keyboard Properties window

In general, you should leave the keyboard settings in their default position. Changing them can cause a real headache and accidently disable your keyboard.

Computer keyboards are very similar to their typewriter ancestors. Their alphabetic keys are set up the same as standard typewriters and most, if not all, computer keyboards also contain a ten-key placed at the side. What makes a computer keyboard different is the addition of some extra keys. Let's take a closer look at some of these special keys.

The Function Keys: These are a group of keys usually found at the top of the keyboard. They are all labeled with an "**F**" plus a number, mostly ranging from 1 to 12. These keys are meant to execute a particular function or program when pressed, depending on which application is running at the time. For instance, with Windows 95, pressing the **F1** key will start the Help program.

The Alt key: The Alt key is found on the bottom of the keyboard, usually beside the space bar. This key's name stands for Alternate and it has a few miscellaneous functions. It is mostly used in Windows to jump up to the menu bar. It is also used commonly in conjunction with other keys, like when using *Alt+Tab*.

The Ctrl key: The Ctrl key is usually found near the Alt key and as you may have guessed, its name stands for Control. The Ctrl key also provides many miscellaneous functions and works in conjunction with other keys, like when using *Ctrl+Esc*. In addition, the Ctrl key can be used like a shift key for releasing those special symbols found underneath certain keys, like *Ctrl+Break* (the Pause key).

The Esc key: The Esc key is designed to get you out of tricky situations, like when a computer locks up. With early computers, the Esc key would simply reset the entire machine. But, in today's world, this key merely acts as a program terminator. Unfortunately, due to complicated operating systems, this key does not always work. That is why "*Ctrl+Alt+Delete*" was invented and if that doesn't do it, you can always push the reset button on exterior of the computer.

The **Delete key** and **Backspace key**: Both these keys share a similar function, they erase mistakes. The only difference between the two, is where they erase. When pressing the Delete key, any mistake made <u>in front of</u> (or to the right of) the cursor will disappear. Whereas, with the Backspace key, any mistake made <u>behind</u> (or to the left of) the cursor will disappear. Either key can erase any highlighted material.

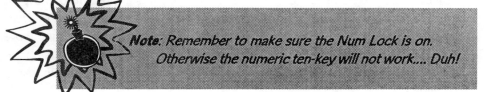

Note: Remember to make sure the Num Lock is on. Otherwise the numeric ten-key will not work... Duh!

Networks, Modems, Mail and Fax

These icons mainly control all the outgoing data sent through modems. They are responsible for all external means of communication. They are only present if a computer has a modem. The modem itself, the hardware device, is discussed further in **Chapter 15**. As for its software properties, they are located within the Control Panel.

Figure 7.10
The Modem Properties window

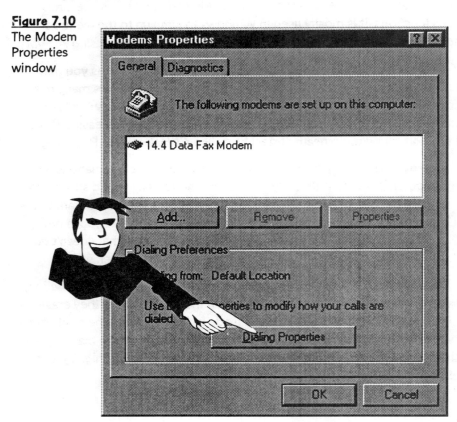

Since other programs can use the modem as well. It is important to know which **COM** port your modem is on. You can find this information in the Modems Properties window by clicking on the **Diagnostics** section, as pointed out above. The COM ports are often a good spot for communication conflicts. By using the modem properties, you can solve most of the software problems surrounding lost communication.

Mouse

The **Mouse icon** in the Control Panel is a lot like the Joystick icon. It allows you to set up the mouse cursor and then proceed to test it. For more information about Mice in general, check out **Chapter 9**.

Multimedia

This topic is also covered in another chapter. It is where Windows 95 takes advantage of today's multimedia technology. Subsequently, if your computer does not have a CD-ROM then the Multimedia icon will be missing. In either case, you will want to read **Chapter 14**.

Passwords

Windows 95 has the ability to deal with passwords. Besides the obvious role, this also inherently lets any computer handle multiple users. Multiple users allow one computer to act like a network. Except, every users uses the same computer, but at different times.

In order to have multiple users, there must be passwords. By allowing each user a password it gives them a separate session in Windows. If this seems too confusing or not exactly your idea of passwords, then you should check out the **Tricks, Hints and Traps** in **Chapter 18**.

Printers

We have seen the Printers before in **Chapter 4** and their appearance in the Control Panel is the same. Clicking on the **Printers icon** in the Control Panel will get you to the same place as clicking on Settings option in the Start up menu and then selecting Printers.

Figure 7.11
The Printers window

Although the diagram above shows six printers, it does not mean there are six printers attached to this system. The icons in this window only represent drivers, not actual printers. In this window, you are allowed to choose the driver you wish to use. Each driver specializes in a particular feature. One driver is made for color prints while another may work well with images. Each drivers does not have to have one to one correspondence with a physical printer.

Of course, this is assuming you own a printer. Windows 95 is compatible with many printers. For a complete list, simply double-click on the **Add Printer** icon.

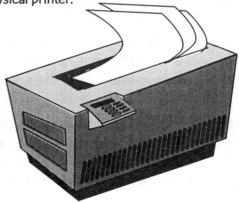

Regional Settings

Windows 95 is a very universal program. It is used in all parts of the world utilizing many different languages, measuring systems, currencies and many other assets of different cultures. To allow this unique relationship to survive, Windows itself must be very adaptable and it is.

Regional Settings

In the Control Panel there is an icon named **Regional Settings**. This icon represents part of the great flexibility of Windows 95. To gain a better understand, double-click on it.

Figure 7.12
The Regional Settings Properties window

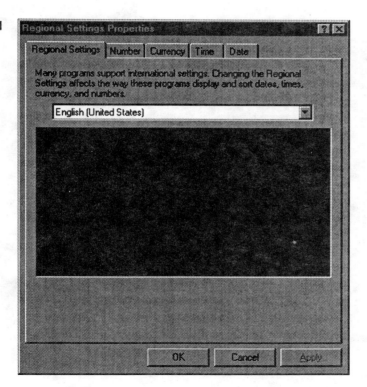

The window shown above is most useful for global travelers or laptop users. It is designed to change the keyboard layout and certain elements of a system, like the time. Although, this window may be interesting, it is not a good window to play around with it. Most of its functions affect the keyboard more than the screen and abusing it may give you a French keyboard by mistake.

Sounds

The **Sounds** in Windows 95 are set up to add character to any computer. They include customary beeps and chimes, which can almost go unnoticed. Although, these sound are designed to get our attention, users seldom ignore them, simply because they sound so familiar and appropriate.

There are some special sounds which may not have been loaded during the initial installation of Windows 95. To obtain these extra sounds, you will need to load them using the **Add/Remove programs** in the Control Panel. We have used this program before, at the beginning of this chapter. Now, we are going to use it to load additional Windows software. This is done in the **Windows Setup** section.

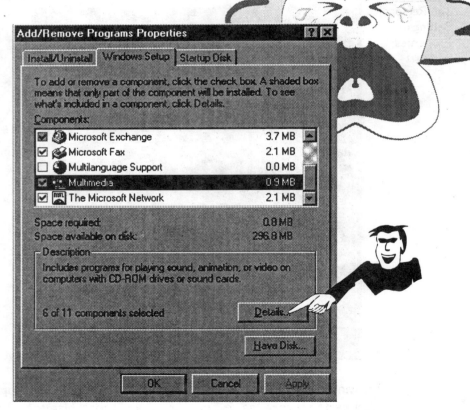

Figure 7.13
The Windows SetUp section of the Add/Remove Programs

In the **Windows Setup**, simply scroll down to the **Multimedia** section and click on the **Detail...** button, as pointed out in the picture above.

This allows you to see a new list of Multimedia components. You will want to scroll down to the bottom of the list until you find a collection of the sounds. There are a total of four extra sounds described as **Sound Schemes**. They include: Jungle sounds, Musica sounds, Robotz sounds and Utopia sounds. Simply put a check (✓) next to each sound and click **OK**, as shown below.

Figure 7.14
Adding extra sounds

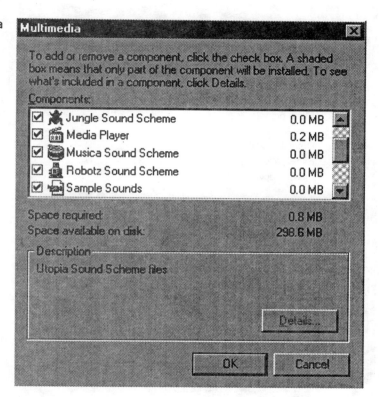

(Subsequently, in addition to the sounds, you can also load extra wallpaper, more utilities or even a few games! Examine each selection using the **Details...** button and take what you want.)

Loading these sounds will not take long, because they only consist of a few files. Once loaded, you will have to go back to the Control Panel and double-click on the **Sounds** icon. This will allow you to use the sounds you just loaded.

The Sounds Property window controls all the noise you hear in Windows 95. Everything from that "*Don't Delete Me!*" sound to the ever-so popular Windows chime is processed in this window. One of the fun parts about this program is it allows you to pick the sounds for any event.

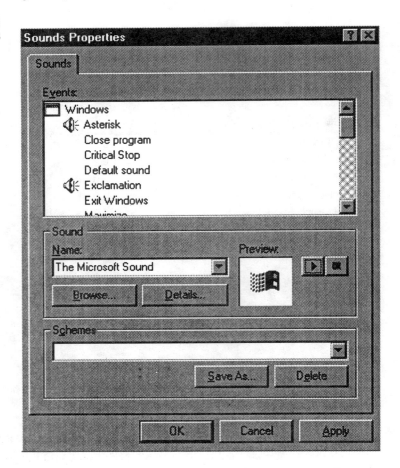

Figure 7.15
The Sounds Property window

Start by selecting an event, like a **Critical Stop** and then choose an appropriate sound by clicking on the **Browse...** button. Furthermore, you should see the extra sounds we previously loaded. This window also lets you sample any sound by pressing the **play** button.

When done, click on **OK** and enjoy the new collection of sounds. Remember, these sounds can be changed at any time, so there is no reason to feel any pressure from not exploring.

System

The **System** icon, in the Control Panel, is basically a technical description of any computer. Most of this information is somewhat specific and could be a bit intimidating at first. So, if the sight of blood or circuits does not bother you, then you can feel pretty safe about clicking on its icon. Otherwise enter with caution, because this is unchartered territory for most amateur users!

Figure 7.16
The System Properties window

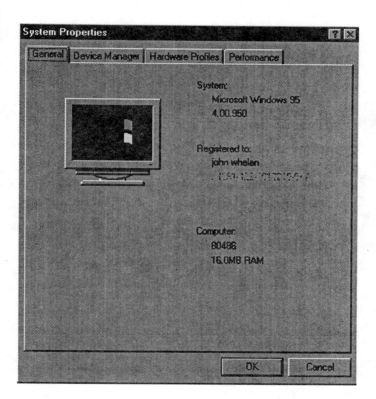

The Introductory window shown above, called **General**, is quite straightforward. It gives a quick portrait of a computer. The information on this window would be the same as if you were describing your system to a friend. Included here, is the official Windows version number (**4.0...**) and your personal Windows ID number.

In the diagram above the personal Windows ID number has been wiped out to protect the author. Any attempt to decipher it is strictly forbidden!

The next window appears when you click on the tab marked **Device Manager**. This window does a more in-depth job of describing the computer. It includes all the internal cards, devices, drives, ports and controllers.

Here is where you can make system changes by adding or removing components. If you are inexperienced at working with a computer, this window is not a good place to practice. The Device Manager is a real component of your system and can do real damage.

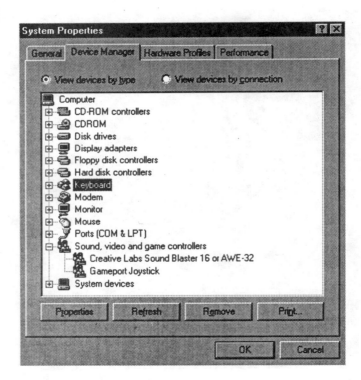

Figure 7.17
The Device Manager in the System Properties window

The Device Manger can be viewed in two ways, by **type** or **connection**. Both views essentially show the same thing. However, view by connection includes all the links which connect each component. This view can be a little more helpful, since you can see what components affect each other.

To access a component, simply click on it. Some components are hidden, so be prepared to do some searching. For example, inquiring about a joystick would be done by clicking on a game controller first. Then clicking on the joystick would eventually open up a properties window for it.

The division called **Hardware profiles** is a safe one to skip. It is rarely used, even by computer nerds. Its main purpose is to allow users to have different hardware setups on their system, this way Windows would load different drivers for different profiles.

The last division of the System Properties window is set aside for the system's performance. It is like a report card for the computer.

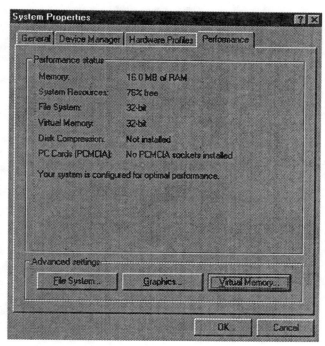

Figure 7.18
The Preformance division of the System Properties window

This window gives a reading of the system's well-being. The main ingredient is the *System Resources*. It tells how much **RAM** is currently used by Windows. This number should almost always be above **70** percent. If it happens to go below **50** percent, you should quit all the programs and restart your computer.

Besides the general performance, this window also lets you modify your system. This can be done by selecting **File System...** and **Virtual Memory...**. Now, if this looks too technical then don't worry, because Windows 95 does it automatically for you and there is no reason to try to improve it. But, for those people who feel they can do a better job than Windows, this is the place where they can prove it.

The Display

CHAPTER 8

With so many Windows users today, sometimes it is very difficult to make one computer stand apart from others. To avoid this problem, Windows 95 includes a program which helps you customize the appearence of its display. This is achieved through a program called the **Display**, which is found in the Control Panel. This program very easy to use and has a great effect on the overall appearance of Windows 95. Although this program has its limitations, I think you will find using it, can make any computer look unique.

For the most part, Windows 95 has an extremely different appearance than its predecessors. Compared to them, Windows 95 concentrates more heavily on wallpaper and less on the appearance of windows. You will remember the wallpaper in earlier versions of Windows was mostly hidden. This isn't true with Windows 95.

The responsibility of managing the appearance of Windows 95 belongs to a small section of the **Control Panel**, in a program called the **Display**. This program is divided into four categories.

Display

① **Background**
② **Screen Savers**
③ **Appearance**
④ **Settings**

Each one of these categories affects a different aspect of the appearance of Windows 95. From colors to sizes, everything is taken into consideration. This allows users to customize their systems and develop a look as unique as they are. However, there are some characteristics in the display which cannot be altered. They are "hard" coded into Windows and are not accessible for users to make changes to them (like certain fonts, icons and windows).

In this chapter, I examine each category of the display and explain how to fully take advantage of their unique features. I believe you should find this very useful and perhaps a little fun. Let's start with the background, or what most people call, wallpaper.

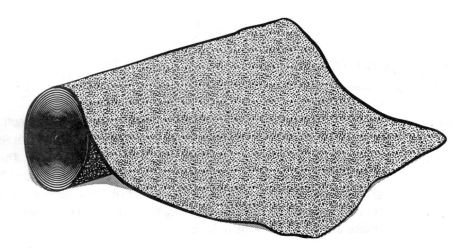

Background

What is wallpaper? Wallpaper in computer terms is analogous to wallpaper in real life. Similar to that stuff which covers most of your bedrooms and hallways. The wallpaper in Windows 95 also covers something, it covers the screen. So instead of seeing some boring colors, confusing windows or nothing at all; we use wallpaper to make the operating system look more attractive and less intimidating.

In a nutshell, wallpaper is a simple picture which covers the background of the screen. There is nothing complicated about it. Wallpaper comes in many different designs, from simple patterns to fascinating pictures. Windows 95, itself comes with a standard section of preloaded wallpaper, everything from castle bricks to zig zags.

So what makes something wallpaper? Wallpaper in Windows are graphic files, commonly found on a hard drive. To become wallpaper, a file only has to possess two criteria.

① The file has to be a **bitmap** (a graphic file containing the extension **.BMP**)
② The file has to reside in the Windows directory on the C drive (**C:\Windows**) or its path.

Furthermore, many commercial programs also come with wallpaper as well. It is even possible to use real photos in your wallpaper. As you can see, the potential is endless and is a lot more exciting then the boring wallpaper you may use at home.

If you do like the idea of adding wallpaper to your computer screen, then feel free to do so. It only takes a couple of seconds and if you don't like the changes you make, then you can always undo them.

Here's how to start redecorating your Windows 95 landscape:

❶ Start with opening up the Display program, by clicking on the **Display** icon found in the **Control Panel**. This will launch the Display Properties window. This window is used to control what you see. It is divided into four sections, each concentrating on a different property.

❷ The first screen, the **Background**, is mainly responsible for the backdrop of the start-up screen. This consists of two main ingredients, the pattern and the wallpaper. The pattern defines the makeup of unused window surfaces, whereas the wallpaper plays a more visible role.

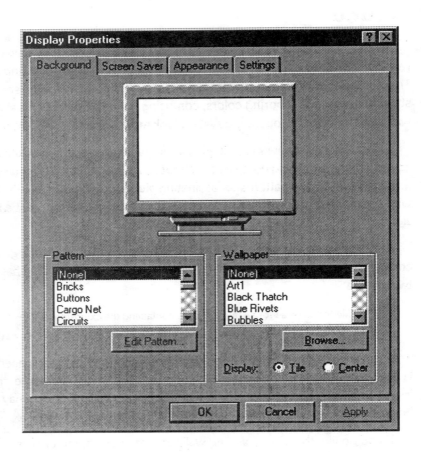

Figure 8.1
The Display Properties window

❸ To change the wallpaper, select the design you want from the list on the *right-hand side* or click on the **Browse...** button to select a design from anywhere outside of the Windows directory (i.e. from a diskette). Doing so, will cause that design to be copied into the Windows directory. Remember, that is one of the requirements for the wallpaper.

❹ To change the pattern, select the pattern you want from the list on the *left-hand side*. There is also an option which allows you to edit a pattern. Personally, I recommend leaving the pattern in its default position, which is **[None]**.

❺ After choosing the appropriate design and/or pattern, select **OK**. That's it. Within a few seconds, your screen's appearance will take on an entire new look.

There are two different ways wallpaper can be displayed, as a **Tile** or in the **Center**. When a design is intended to be drawn multiple times over the entire screen in a tile-like fashion, it is known as a tile pattern, not to be confused, with the patterns discussed on the previous page. It is important to select the tile option when using these types of designs for wallpaper; otherwise, the wallpaper could result in a small square placed in the middle of the screen.

On the other hand, the center option works well with big pictures and anything which is not a simple repetitive design, because it places them in the middle of the screen. In either case you can try both options out for yourself to see which works best.

After a little exploring, you will probably find most of the designs Microsoft provides to be ample at best. They are pretty elementary and get easily tiresome. Fortunately, Windows 95 allows its user to make their own wallpaper.

To make your own wallpaper, all you need is a graphics program which produces a bitmap. Graphics programs that produce bitmaps, may sound complicated, but they don't always have to be. A simple graphic program which will work is included within Windows 95. It is a program called **Paint**, and I examine it in greater detail in **Chapter 11**.

Using your own creations may not be the best way to make your wallpaper look appealing. Instead, try using other people's creations (i.e. pictures). One way of finding these creations is by searching your hard drive for all the **.BMP** files. Once you find a file (picture) you like, simply move it to the windows directory (instructions on moving files are found in the **My Computer & Explorer Chapter**).

Screen Savers

What is a screen saver? You have probably seen them before on computers, and you might even know what they do. But, why do they do what they do?

Figure 8.2
A Screen Saver

A screen saver is a small program which executes when the computer is inactive, meaning the computer has not received any input for a period of time. For example, if you leave your computer to get a drink of water and then return. You might find strange figures are dancing around the screen, that's a screen saver. Many companies make screen savers which you can purchase, not to mention, Windows 95 itself comes with a few.

The reasoning behind screen savers is a little outdated. Older systems with obsolete monitors use to suffer from a crippling disease known as **screen burn**. Screen burn occured anytime an image was on a screen for too long. The image would actually burn into the screen, so remnants of that image could still be seen, even though the image itself was gone. To fix this problem, programmers created flashy screen savers.

Screen burn was blamed on a series of problems, from old colorless monitors to boring text screens. Presently, with the advent of new monitors and more active screens, screen burn itself has become extinct. Consequently, even though they don't serve any useful function, screen savers are more popular today than ever.

All the screen savers in Windows 95 are managed by one program, even if they are made by different companies. Activating a screen saver is a lot like selecting wallpaper, they both reside in the Display Properties window. Once in this window, you need to click on the **Screen Saver** tab at the top. This gives you complete control over all the screen savers in Windows.

Figure 8.3
Selecting a
Screen Saver

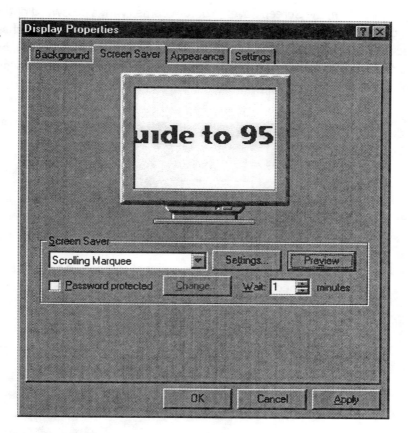

Unlike the wallpaper, the list of screen savers is automatically provided and cannot be changed by a user. Although it can't be changed, it is frequently updated by Windows to allow other programs to add their screen savers.

When selecting a screen saver, you are also allowed to choose the interval time. This is the time the computer has to remain inactive, for the screen saver to start. If this time is too short, like one or two minutes, your screen saver will start practically every time you turn your head. This could be a little irritating. On the other hand, if you set the time for too long, like 20 or 30 minutes, then you may never get to experience your screen saver at all. Therefore it is best to pick a time interval which isn't too short, nor too long. I suggest trying 5 minutes.

In addition, the Screen Saver program comes with a password option. To use it, click on the box next to the word **Password protected**. Then to change or select a password, click on the **Change...** button. This is a nice feature, but it could also be very dangerous. Make sure you remember the correct password, because Windows 95 is very sensitive.

Figure 8.4
Selecting a Password

For the most part, screen savers are optional and do not have to be used. They are really only designed for entertainment purposes.

The Appearance

Up until now, I haven't really discussed altering the true appearance of Windows 95. I have mentioned wallpaper and screen savers, but those two preferences are optional, and really don't affect the look of Windows that much.

Like the wallpaper and the screen saver, the means of changing the appearance reside in the Display program and are accessible by clicking on the **Appearance** tab, at the top of the Display Properties window, as shown below.

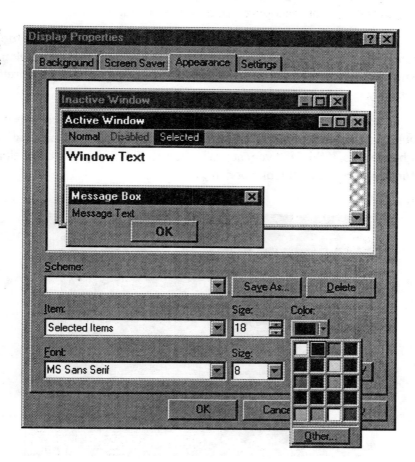

Figure 8.5
Altering the Appearance of windows

The physical appearance of Windows 95 can vary from **27** prefabricated designs, not to mention the designs you can create yourself. These designs range in everything from large lettering to high contrasting colors and are only limited by software coding (for example, you can't change the font on the start button, that has been hard coded).

Microsoft has preloaded designs to help give you a start. From there, you can either choose one of these or make your own. I suggest checking out *Desert*, *Maple*, *Pumpkin (Large)* or *Rainy Day*. As you can see Microsoft went ahead and gave them real descriptive names, not to mention looks.

You can also custom design colors. This option may seem a little too cumbersome, but it is there if you want to utilize it. It basically lets you develop colors which previous didn't exist, though some of these colors can seem pretty unsightly.

To do this, click on the **Other...** option when you go to choose a color. This launches a color generating program, which allows users to create half-tones and other shades. If this isn't very appealing to you, I'm sure you are not alone. Windows 95 does not look good in plaid.

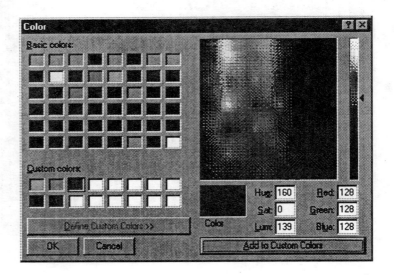

Figure 8.6
Making Colors

Settings

The **Settings** handle the mechanics behind the systems' display. This allows the screen to reach its ideal appearance. In most cases, this will depend greatly on what kind of hardware you are using. Within the Settings window, there are three main divisions; the **Color** palette, the **Desktop** area and the **Font** size.

The **Color** palette shows the total amount of colors the screen can display. The selection can vary, depending on how much memory a video card has. On most computers the minimum is 16 colors, while the average is closer to 256.

The **Desktop** area consists of a little scroll bar, which changes the spacing or size of the desktop. This allows the screen to change its size, without altering any applicable data. In addition, depending upon the size you choose, you can alter the font size respectively.

Figure 8.7
Working with the Display Settings

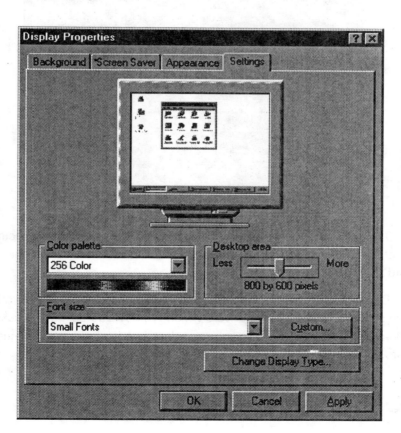

When dealing with the screen's physical appearance, there are two elements you should take into account:

① the **monitor** or its **driver**. Both of these can be packaged together, although they do not have to be.
② and the **video card**.

A driver is a piece of software which helps interpret physical devices. Drivers are very common within Windows and almost every component has one. There are drivers for the keyboard, CD-ROM and so on. The monitor has a driver as well and it is displayed when you click the **Change Display Type...** button.

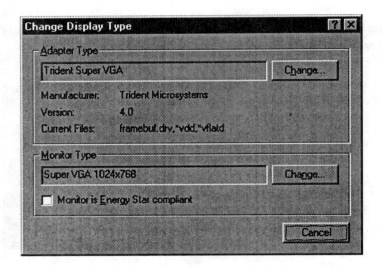

Figure 8.8
Changing the Display and/or the Driver

The window shown above indicates which drivers are presently being used. There are two divisions, one for the driver (or as windows calls it, the adapter) and another for the monitor.

Depending upon which monitor you own, decides which driver your system can support. To see a list of drivers which Windows 95 supports, click on the **Change...** button. From here you can select a particular driver or a generic Windows driver.

The Mouse

CHAPTER 9

The mouse is one tool which has helped make Windows into a great operating system and has done the same thing for many other programs, as well. In general, mice have been a standard part of computing since the eighties, and their purpose and design have not changed much. They also have a considerable role to play in Windows 95 and their significance tends to go completely unnoticed or unrecognized. This is why I have dedicated this entire chapter to them.

What is a mouse?

In most cases, a mouse would be a rodent which possesses gnawing teeth, a somewhat pointed snout and a sparsely haired tail. This is the kind of mouse you would expect to find in a sewer, not in a computer book. Which is why I'm going to talk about the other kind of mouse, the ones computers use.

In computer terms, a mouse is simply an input device, much like a keyboard. It helps translate the external world into bits and bytes for the computer. Like all input devices, the mouse becomes an additional extension used to gain a better grasp on any computer's potential.

For the most part, there are two kinds of mice; **bus** mice and **serial** mice. Both kinds work the same way. The main difference between them is the plug at the end of the cord. A bus mouse is distinguished by its circular end, whereas a serial mouse's end would be rectangular. Taking this into account, both kinds of mice would have to plug into different places on the back end of a computer. So depending upon which kind of mouse your system can support, will give you a pretty good idea of which kind of mouse you own.

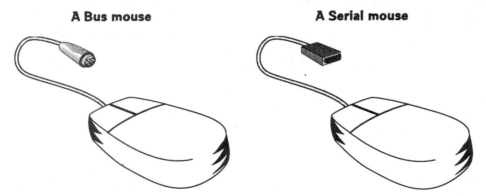

Another important aspect about a mouse, is how it communicates with the computer. When the mouse is moved, it sends a signal to the CPU. This signal is called an **interrupt** and it is a way of getting the CPUs attention. As you can imagine the CPU gets a lot of these signals. Fact is, every device on the computer can cause (or send) an interrupt.

To avoid **collisions** or **conflicts**, these interrupts are prioritized within the computer. Important interrupts, like the reset button, are given the highest priority. Devices which are used a lot, also have a significant amount of priority to accommodate for their usage.

In addition, each kind of mice, bus or serial, have unique priorities, as well. Because their priorities are <u>not</u> the same, the nature of their configuration can cause potential conflict problems to arise, depending upon which kind of mouse is used. Frequently, serial mice are more inclined to cause conflicts.

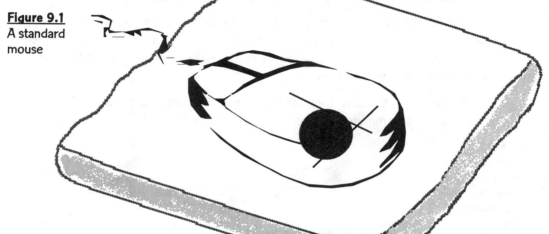

Figure 9.1
A standard mouse

In general, almost all mice consist of two main parts; a small rubber ball and a housing unit for that ball. When you move a mouse, the small ball inside it moves as well. The movement of this ball causes two bars perpendicular to each other to rotate. Then a sensor within the mouse detects the movement of these bars and sends a signal to the CPU.

Considering this, it is not important how clean you keep that ball, since it really never touches any sensors. This is also why mice seem to work well in any environment, with or without a mouse pad. As long as that ball can move, regardless of how well, a mouse will have no problem functioning.

I am sure this is more than you ever wanted to know about a mouse, but it can never hurt to know too much. I am sure, this kind of information will prove to be useful if you are encountering problems with your mouse and have to do some troubleshooting.

Working with a mouse

One of the requirements for Windows 95 is a mouse. Most, if not all, systems sold today come with one of them. Mice are everywhere and have proven to be a permanent part of the computer architecture. In the past, Windows have depended heavily on them, even though you could have feasibly gotten away without owning one. Presently, with Windows 95, the absence of a mouse will make the operating system seem very dull and completely useless. After all, when in comes to Windows, clicking is the only way to get something done.

Mice in Windows act very strange. Sometimes they are hard to find, or sometimes they are hard to control. In either case, they seem to have a mind of their own. Learning how to control a mouse is worth the effort and will make you a more effective Windows user.

To start with, the movement of a mouse isn't as unpredictable as you might think. Take a few minutes to examine the diagrams below and on the next page.

Figure 9.2
The slower a mouse is moved, the less distance its cursor covers on the screen.

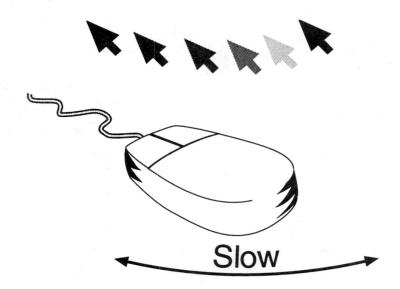

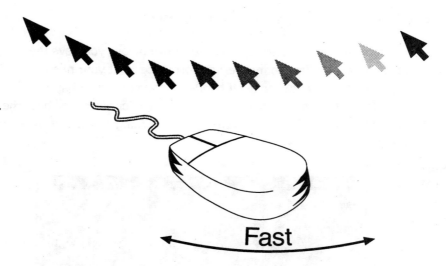

Figure 9.3
The faster a mouse is moved, the further its cursor moves on the screen.

Therefore, the speed at which a mouse is moved has a great effect on the amount of distance it can cover on the screen. This gives the mouse a great amount of freedom, even in tight places.

In general, a standard mouse has two buttons on it, one on the left and another on the right. Some mice include an extra button, which acts as a double-click.

The left button, which is usually the larger than the right, acts as the main initiator for the mouse. Originally when developed, there was only one button designed for the mouse. However, as its role progressed, its creators realized most functions could not be explored with the use of just one button, so the "double-click" was invented and soon after an additional button was added altogether.

Another way to have more control over a mouse in Windows, is to customized it. By changing the look or the speed of a mouse, you can gain greater control of it. To do this, we need to look in the **Control Panel** for the **Mouse** icon. This icon opens the **Mouse Properties** window.

The Mouse Properties window

In the Mouse Properties window, shown below, you have the ability to customize the mouse's performance to fit your needs. You can choose between a left-handed mouse or a right-handed one. The first screen also lets you work on its "clicking" abilities. The speed which is mentioned in this window refers to the clicking speed, not the overall speed of the mouse.

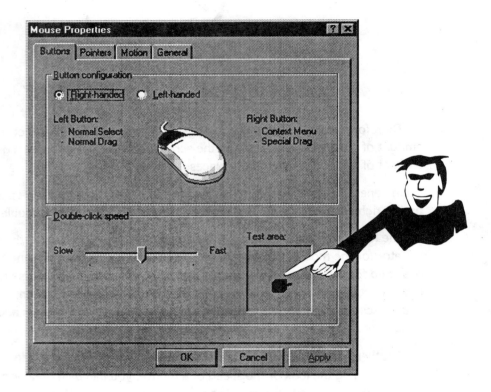

Figure 9.4
The Mouse Properties window

In general, try not to make the mouse's clicking speed too fast. Since the faster the clicking speed is, the faster you have to double-click the mouse. On the other hand, slowing down the clicking speed has little or no effect on the mouse at all. In both cases, you are given an object to test on. It is clearly identified as the **Test area**, as pointed out above.

The Mouse

The **second** screen of the Mouse Properties window, accessible by clicking on the **Pointers** tab, allows you to change the appearance of the mouse cursor in Windows. This lets you decide what the mouse will look like on your screen.

Figure 9.5
The Pointers section of the Mouse Properties window

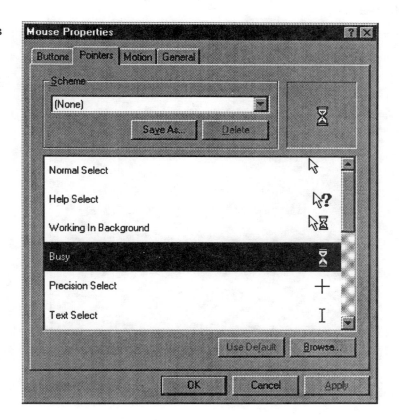

The window shown above displays all the different appearances of a mouse cursor can have. A mouse cursor changes its look to show what the computer (CPU) is doing. If a computer is busy processing or thinking the mouse cursor has a certain look to show that.

To change the appearance of the mouse, select the style of mouse you want to change and click on the **Browse...** button. Then you can pick from a selection of different cursors. In addition, you can also buy extension programs which have a larger selection of cursors to choose from.

This window is a good place to visit, after first installing Windows 95. It allows you to make Windows screen look like, it was not just taken out of the box.

The third screen of the Mouse Properties window, accessible by clicking on the **Motion** tab, allows you to change the movement of the mouse cursor. To speed up the reaction time of a mouse, just slide the speed-bar to the appropriate speed.

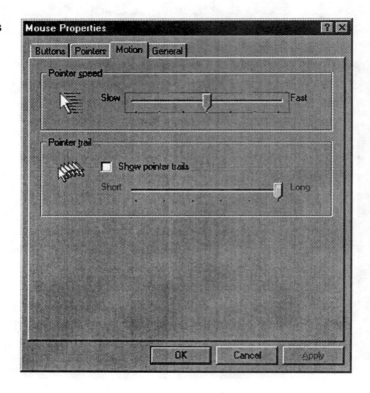

Figure 9.6
The Motions section of the Mouse Properties window

Although this screen may seem a lot like the first screen of the Mouse Properties window, its functionality is a lot different. In this screen you are working with the movement of the mouse itself, not its clicking speed.

I strongly suggest keeping the mouse speed in the middle, meaning not too low or not too high. If you slow the mouse down too much, it will take forever to reach its destination on the screen. Subsequentially, if you speed its motion up too much, you will not be able to accurately control it. In either case, you might end up clicking or starting on the wrong programs.

The last screen of the Mouse Properties window, accessible by clicking on the **General** tab, provides you with basic information about your mouse.

If you were going to change your mouse to a different kind, this would be a good place to start. Or if you were experiencing some problems with the mouse you currently own, this window could help out a lot, as well. Otherwise, this window is best left untouched.

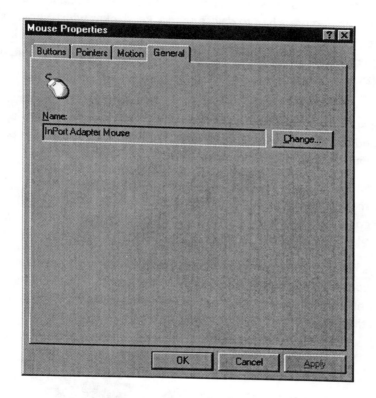

Figure 9.7
The last screen on the Mouse Properties window

Mice can take a fair amount of abuse, considering how technical they are. Unlike other electronic components, mice rarely need physical attention and can go easily unnoticed; that is until someone takes one away. Then most users turn to jelly and seem to lose their way around the screen.

But, the loss of a mouse does have to be an end-all situation. There may be times when a mouse refuses to work, or is temporarily damaged. In these cases, you can actually use the keyboard as a mouse!

"Clicking the keyboard"

Yes, there is life with out a mouse. Even though a mouse is a requirement for Windows 95, there are situations where you can get away without having one. Because computers were invented long before the mouse, the mouse has had to evolve around them, slowly making its presence known.

Since, there was a time when some computers had mice and others didn't, program manufacturers had to devise special keystrokes which simulated mouse movements. These special keystrokes were often a combinations of keys which otherwise wouldn't have been used as much. For example, they would use the *arrow keys* to move the mouse pointer.

This became so popular, a standard was developed for computers without mice. A set of special keystrokes was put set aside for the mouse, to simulate its movements and abilities. These keystrokes are still available today and can be used on any computer supporting Windows.

In addition, because keyboard commands can be more precise than the clicking of a mouse, they are often a better alternative with many programs. It is very easy to confuse a computer with rapid mouse movements or some quick clicking. In general, most computers simply can't keep up with most mice.

However, using a keyboard eliminates these kind of problems. This is because most keyboards have a direct connection to the computer, though its motherboard. Unlike the mouse which must go through a controller first, before it ever reaches the CPU.

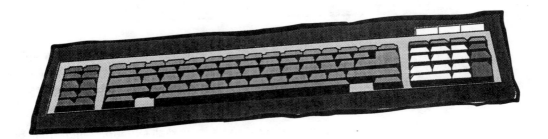

The table below outlines the most common keystrokes used today and their functions. Each keystroke is designed to simulate a different movement of a mouse. Many of these keystrokes can be used in conjunction with each other, as well as with an functional mouse.

Keystrokes	What it does
The **Arrow** keys	Simulates the movement of the mouse pointer, when possible.
The **Enter** key	Acts like a "double-click".
The **Spacebar**	Acts like a "single-click".
The **Tab** key	Selects the next option in a window or dialog box
The **Shift+Tab** key	Selects the next option, but in the opposite direction (i.e. it reverses what the Tab key does).
The **Alt** key	Selects the Menu bar.

The degree to how well these special keystrokes work depend heavily upon the situations they are used in. In addition, you may want to reexamine the **keyboard** section of Chapter 7 or check out **hint #2** in the Helpful hints section of Chapter 18.

Working With Windows 95

I want My Windows 3.1 Back!

CHAPTER 10

Some users might be a little sadded with the arrival of Windows 95. Many of them may have simply grown accustomed to the earlier versions of Windows and could hesitate when it comes to upgrading. However, to help ease some of this pain, Microsoft has included within Windows 95 links to some of its earlier programs. This allows both new and old users to appreciate Windows 95 in whatever environment they were familiar with. For that reason, I have designed this chapter to show you new ways of getting old programs back.

Getting Back the old File Manager

The **File Manager** has been a landmark of Windows since its early days. It has been a dependable program which was used to examine the entire computer and all the files within it.

With Windows 95, the File Manager was replaced by two newer programs, called **My Computer** and the **Windows Explorer**. Although, these programs provide essentially the same functions as the File Manager, they are not as complete or as thorough as their predecessor. In addition, many users have plainly grown accustomed to the layout of the File Manager. There is no reason to hide the fact that some parts of Window 3.1 are difficult to forget.

Luckily for us, the File Manager is still somewhat accessible in Windows 95. Microsoft made sure Windows 95 didn't destroy any important programs, during its initial installation. This included the File Manager.

The only problem with the File Manager in Windows 95 is trying to locate it. Since it no longer has an icon or a window to inhabit, the File Manager may go completely unseen. In fact, the only part of the File Manager which still remains is the file itself. However, by copying this file to a more accessible location, the glory days of the File Manager can be redeemed.

To accomplish this, a copy of the File Manager must be moved into a more familiar place, like the Start up screen or in the Start menu. Doing this is easier than it sounds and can be accomplished in a few seconds. The steps below outline how this can be done.

❶ The first step is to locate the executable file for the **File Manager**. The file is called **Winfile** and it is located in the **Windows directory**.

To find it, click on the **My Computer** icon and work your way down to the Windows directory (i.e. click on the "**C**" drive then click on the **Windows directory**). **Winfile** should be located towards the end of the Windows directory, since the directory is alphabetized by file names. You will know you have found the right file, because accompanying it will be a small icon with a picture of a file cabinet.

Winfile

Figure 10.1
Finding the File Manager (Winfile)

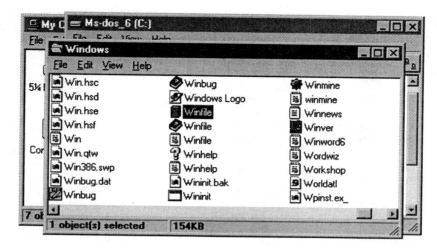

❷ The next step is to make a copy of this file and put it in a more accessible place. To do this, start with selecting the file by clicking on it. Then drag it off the window and place it on the **Start** button, the **Taskbar** or the **Desktop**. Doing this will essentially copy the file and put somewhere easier to access. This does not cause any harm to the computer and the location of this file, because you are only making copies of it and not moving it entirely.

Figure 10.2
Placing the Winfile in the Start menu

Placing the Winfile on the Start button, will effectively make a shortcut of the Winfile in the Start menu. This allows you to access this file in the same manner as you would with the other Programs, Documents, Settings, Find, Help and Run buttons.

Figure 10.3
The New Start up menu

❸ Once the file has been placed on the Start button, you can rename it from "Winfile" to its original name, "File Manager". This is fairly easy to do within the Taskbar Properties window and here's how:

☑ First, from the Taskbar Properties windows, click on the Start Menu Programs tab.
☑ Then click on the **Advance...** button.

Figure 10.4
The Start Menu Programs of the Taskbar Properties window

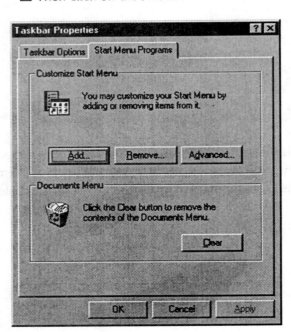

☑ Next, locate the Winfile and rename it. This is done by highlighting the file and pressing the "**F2**" key, as shown below.

Figure 10.5
Renaming the Winfile

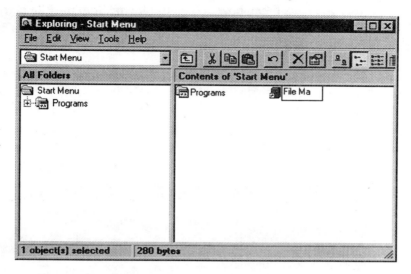

☑ Finally, click the **OK** button to save the changes.

Now the same procedure can be followed with the old **Program Manager** as well. Just follow the same steps, only instead of using the Winfile, you will want to use the executable file for the Program Manager, which is called **Progman** and it too is located in the **Windows directory**. After a little work, your Windows 95 start up menu will look a little more customary and familiar.

After a little work, you can customize the Start menu so it includes programs from the past and present. This will make any computer into a universal system, spanning both geographical boundaries, as well as historical ones.

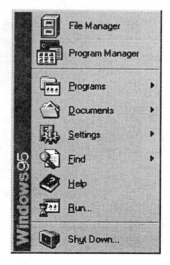

Using the File Manager and Program Manager

Now that you have them, how do you use them? Both the **File Manager** and **Program Manager** operate the same as they did in previous versions of Windows, granted they may look a little different.

Take the Program Manager for example. This use to be the backbone of Windows. Actually a lot of people thought it was Windows. However, in Windows 95, the presence of the Program Manager takes on a new role. Now it is a separate application, rather than the central program overseeing everything. To get the full picture, you need to start the Program Manager and see it for yourself.

Figure 10.6
The Program Manager inside of Windows 95

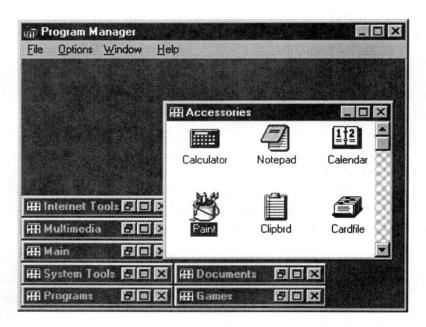

In Windows 95, the Program Manager is a <u>tool</u> and is not meant to be used as the main window in the computer, like it was in early versions. In fact, when installing new software, the Program Manager's contents will <u>not</u> automatically update, like it use to. Instead, you will have to create an icon for every new program installed (for instructions on how to do this, you should refer to a Windows 3.1 book).

So how did the Program Manager get filled in the first place? During the initial installation of Windows 95, a copy of all the contents of in the old Program Manager was put in the new Program Manager. From then on, any further additional programs must be added manually to the Program Manager. That is if you want to see them there.

This is one reason the Program Manager is not utilized as often as it use to be. Microsoft wants us to avoid using the Program Manager as much as possible, and use it only as a remembrance. Because someday other newer programs in Windows 95 will supersede these older ones.

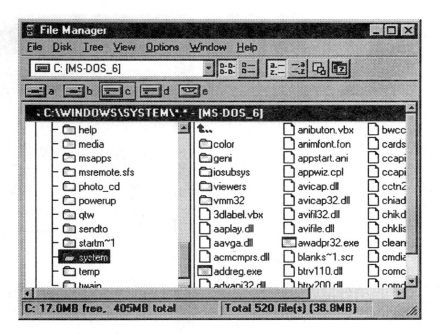

Figure 10.7
The File Manager in Windows 95

As for the **File Manager** in Windows 95, it is much more practical than the Program Manager. The File Manager continues to perform the way it did in previous versions, with only a few minor limitations. It still provides information on files, including file extensions, which makes a great addition to Windows 95.

However, as for its limitations, The File Manager in Windows 95 still has roots from its early days. Therefore, it cannot recognize any file names longer than **8** characters. When it comes across one, the File Manager will replace that part of file's name with a "~" symbol.

A new feature of Windows 95 is the recognition of long file names. In Windows 3.1, a file name was limited to 8 characters. Now with Windows 95, that limit has been pushed to **255** characters. However, because the File Manager is actually an old Windows 3.1 program, it has a hard time with these new long file names.

Although the File Manager's replacements, **My Computer** and the **Windows Explorer** are slightly easier to use, you may find yourself retreating back to the File Manager for its familiarity and crude power.

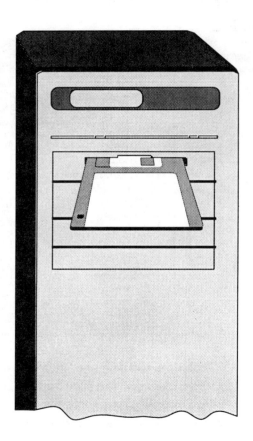

Where is My Task List?

I know you probably think the word "**Task**" is a Windows 95 invention, but I'm sorry to say it isn't. It was really used a lot before in other versions of Windows, although it wasn't advertised as much.

The Task List, use to be a window which displayed a list of all the currently running programs in Windows. Today, in Windows 95, this list is maintained on the **Taskbar**, hence its name. However, if you want to, you can retrieve the old Task List from past versions of Windows. You merely follow the same steps as you would when retrieving the File Manager and the Program Manager. Only this time the name of the executable file is called the **Taskman** and it too is located within the Windows directory.

Figure 10.8
The Task List in Windows 95

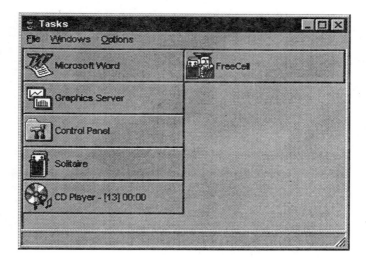

Using the Task List in Windows 95 is quite straight forward. Simply click on the program you want to view. After a while, you should notice the Task List is not really needed, since the Taskbar is right at your finger tips.

We have now customized Windows 95, so both old and new users alike can operate it. From this point on, we will start to look at some new features, unique to Windows 95. Arranging from new games to new ideas; how to find them and how to use them, this will all be covered in the next chapter.

The Ten Pack

CHAPTER 11

This chapter examines ten accessory programs which are included with Windows 95. These programs are not meant to be the bread and butter, but instead are designed to give a sampling of some typical applications. They range from word processors to communication programs and this chapter outlines them all. These programs help make Windows 95 into a complete package, giving it much more flexibility and totality than any other operating system.

The Ten Pack

In actuality, Windows 95 comes with quite a few more than ten accessory programs (it is closer to 19). But the ten I am going to describe in this chapter are considered by most to be the big ones. This means, you will probably use most of these programs more than once in your Windows lifetime. Below is a list of these ten programs.

① Calculator
② Calendar
③ Cardfile
④ Character Map
⑤ Clipboard Viewer
⑥ HyperTerminal
⑦ Notepad
⑧ Paint
⑨ Phone Dialer
⑩ Wordpad

All these programs are located within the **Accessories** folder. If by chance you are missing some of them, don't return your copy of Windows 95 to the retailer just yet.

Because there are a few different ways to install Windows 95, some of these programs may have been absent from your initial installation. So, to give all my readers a fair start, I am going to explain how to install all these programs and many others. The procedure is very similiar to the way we added extra sounds in Chapter 7.

❶ Start by opening the **Control Panel** and clicking on the **Add/Remove Programs** icon. This way, we can add programs which are missing from the original installation. The reason some of these files may be missing is quite simple. Windows wanted to save time during the original installation, so it left some files out.

Add/Remove Programs

❷ The **Add/Remove Programs Properties window** is where Windows decides what collection of programs it will contain. You will want to click on the **Windows Setup** tab, so you can see the selection of programs to choose from. The selection is very large because the audience of Windows 95 is extremely diverse.

Figure 11.1
The Add/Remove Programs Properties window

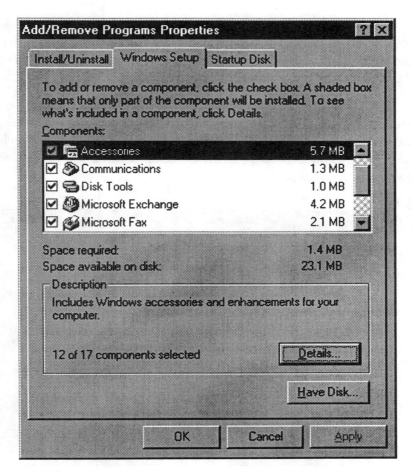

While exploring the selection of programs, put a check (☑) next to the programs you want. Don't forget to inquire further by clicking on the **Details...** button. Otherwise, you may miss some really cool programs.

When finished, click on **OK**. Be sure to have the original Windows 95 diskettes or CD-ROM with you, because you will need them as the additional programs are loaded into the system.

As you can see, Windows 95 has a lot of extra programs which were not displayed on its retail package. The rest of this chapter is design to explore some of them.

Calculator

Calculator

Windows 95, as with previous versions, comes with a **calculator**. It is nothing to write home about, but it does fulfill a useful function. It is very simple to operate and can be used with a mouse or the keypad (*don't forget to make sure the NumLock key is on, when using the ten-key*).

The Calculator works in two modes, **Standard** and **Scientific**. The standard mode is the most useful, because it keeps the calculator from looking too complicated. Nevertheless, take a look at the Scientific mode as well. You might be surprised by Windows' ability to handle complex math. Too bad this calculator can't fit inside your pocket.

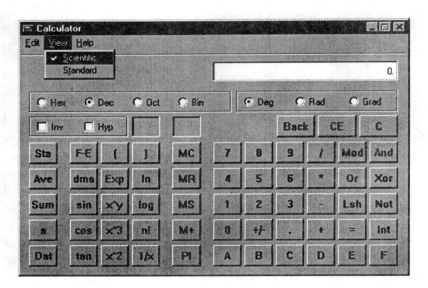

Figure 11.2
Calculator in Scientific Mode

This calculator is not much different than its ancestor, aside from its new Windows 95 metallic look. It has always been an accessory with Windows, because it comes in real handy when you need a quick answer. All of its functions operate exactly like a hand held calculator.

Calendar

The **Calendar**, like the Calculator, has also always been a part of the Windows operating system. In Windows 95, it carries on the tradition of keeping dates and appointments in order and doing it in a rather simple, but effective way.

Calendar

The Calendar works off the system clock which is interconnected to Windows. This allows you to set alarms which can be later displayed on the screen. It is a handy feature and the Calendar as a whole is very easy to operate. Like the Calculator, the Calendar works in two modes, **Day** and **Month**.

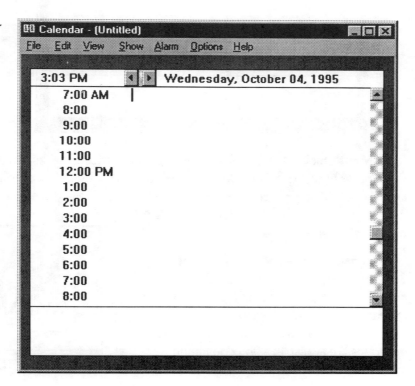

Figure 11.3
The Calendar Program in day mode

In **Day** mode, as shown above, you can enter in descriptions of important events. Although, you will want be careful, because you can't enter any sentences longer than **80** characters. Entering appointments may seem strange at first, but you should keep in mind this program is only meant to be a sample. There are other calendar programs available at computer stores.

Figure 11.4
The Calendar in Month Mode

In **Month** mode, the Calendar takes on a more recognizable appearance. You can quickly toggle to this mode (and back to the Day mode) by pressing the **F9** key. Though Month mode is rather trivial, you always have the option of printing it out to make your own Windows personal pin-up calendar.

In general, the calendar which comes with Windows 95 has many useful features and can be a real time saver. But, if its boring appearance and lack of excitement get to you, then take comfort in knowing other calendar programs are available; if you don't mind spending a little extra cash.

Cardfile

The **Cardfile** is a neat little program which can be very practical. It works much like a real life roll-a-dex or address book by keeping and organizing names of people which are important to you. Since this type of information is real convenient for personal use, keeping it in a computer makes perfect sense.

Cardfile

Like the Calendar, other address book programs can be purchased at any computer store. But, if you want to save some money, try using Microsoft's version, because it does a pretty good job. Let me show you how to use it and I am sure you will agree.

Figure 11.5
The Cardfile Program

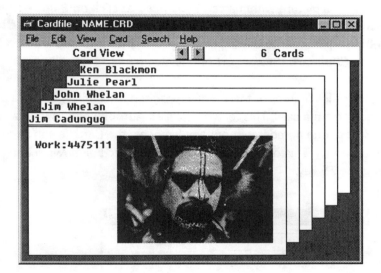

To start things off, begin with giving your Cardfile a **name**. This way you can have different Cardfiles for different occasions, like one for work and another for personal use. Once a Cardfile has been named, all you need to do is fill it up. A Cardfile can hold pictures, sounds or even text files. Here is how you enter a card into your Cardfile.

❶ Adding a card to your Cardfile is simple. Choose **Add** from the **Card** pull-down menu or press the **F7** key.

❷ Next, enter the name of the person or company you wish to add to your list. This will become the title of that particular card. Keep in mind, if you want your list alphabetized by last name, you will want to enter their last name first.

Figure 11.6
Adding a name

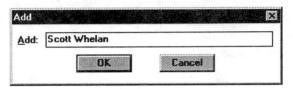

❸ After clicking **OK**, the card will automatically be placed in the correct location. From here all you need to do is provide the phone numbers and addresses.

❹ To include a picture within a card, you need to click on **Picture** from the **Edit** menu. Then paste it from the Clipboard to the card by pressing **Ctrl V**. As for getting a picture into the Clipboard, you will want to skip ahead a few pages to the **Clipboard Viewer** part of this chapter.

Another slick feature of the Cardfile program is its ability to dial a phone number directly from a card. This feature is called **Autodial** and as long as you entered the correct phone number without any hyphens, the Cardfile can become an instant secretary. This option is available in the **Card** pull-down menu or by pressing the **F5** key.

Figure 11.7
Using the Autodialer with the Cardfile

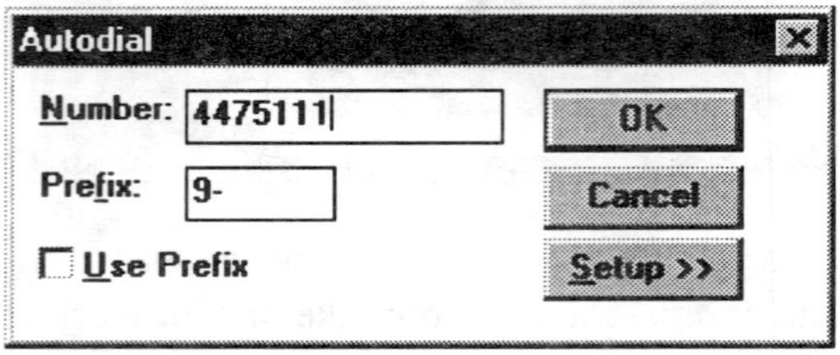

The **Autodialer** itself is just another program included in Windows 95 and as you can see, it has a special relationship with the Cardfile program. In order for this relationship to work certain specifications must be addressed.

When using the autodial feature, you must make sure your system is configured correctly. The key ingredient is the **COM** port. The Autodialer's COM port has to match with the COM port your modem is using.

To find out which **COM** port your modem is using, click on the **modem** icon in the **Control Panel** (i.e. the Modem Properties window). Another important element of the Autodialer is its **speed** and it too should match with your modem's speed. This quality is easier to recognize than the **COM** port, because modems are basically priced by their speed. In any case, these specifications are essential for the relationship between the Autodialer and the Cardfile to work.

After checking the modem properties, you will want to check the specifications of the Autodialer to make sure they match (or are compatible). The Autodialer specifications are found by clicking on the **Setup>>** button, after you choose **Autodial...** from the **Card** pull-down menu.

Figure 11.8
Setting up the COM port

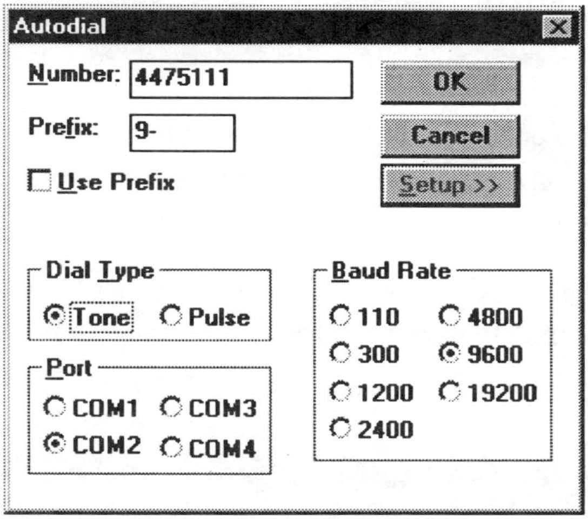

However, with most computers the relationship between the auto-dialer and the modem is set up automatically and presents less of a worry, if you purchased your computer with the modem pre-installed. Otherwise, after a quick check, you should be able to use this great feature and not have to worry about looking at any of these numbers again. As for the Autodialer, it will be discussed in greater detail later on in this chapter.

The Cardfile also has many unique features as well. There is a searching option which helps find entries, in case your Cardfile gets to large. You also have the ability to view the Cardfile as a list. This way it is easier to see its entire contents.

Character Map

Character Map

The **Character Map** is a strange program and few users ever really utilize it. Its lack of popularity can be blamed on two things. First, many users don't understand how to use it and secondly it does not have a great deal of useful applications. The Character Map is a lot like the royal family in England; neither really fill a useful role (I guess, that's being a little harsh on the Character Map).

The Character Map was designed to let users access special kinds of characters, such as © ± ñ ™ or ¢. These characters are very helpful when writing in foreign languages or using mathematical equations. There is a different map of characters for every **font** on the system.

Each map then allows any of its characters to be selected, copied and then used. Though this sequence may seem a little odd at first, as soon as you use it a few times, it becomes quite a simple chore. Keep in mind, you may never have to use the Character Map at all, so don't let its oddities discourage you.

Here is how you use the Character Map:

❶ First, start the program, by clicking on its icon within the **Accessories** folder. Then select the correct font from the list. For the example below, we will use *Times New Roman*.

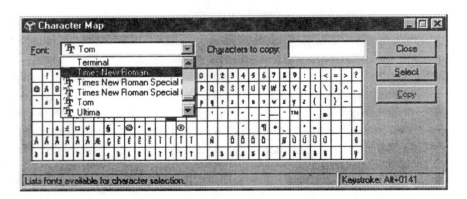

Figure 11.9
Selecting a font

❷ The next step is to pick a character you wish to apply. For this example, we are going to select an "â" symbol. So, we can write our buddies in France.

❸ After choosing the character, in this case the "á" symbol, click on the **Select** button. This officially selects the character and prepares it to be copied. You will notice a copy of it has been moved to the **Characters to copy:** box.

Figure 11.10
Selecting a character

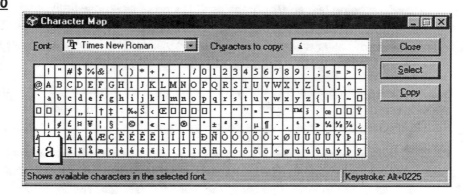

❹ Next you will want to click on the **Copy** button. This copies the character into the Clipboard, so you can use it in your document (or letter).

Now, to use that character, you need to copy it from the Clipboard to your document (or letter). One way of doing this, is by using the copy command (pressing **Ctrl+V**). So, with our example, every time we press **Crtl+V** an "á" symbol will appear.

The Character Map is very useful when you want to include fancy characters in any of your documents. In fact, Windows has dedicated an entire font just for fancy characters, it's called *Wingdings*. You really should take some time to check this font out. It may come in handy with resumes and other important documents.

*Note: In the bottom right-hand corner of the Character Map there is some unusual text. It says something like, Keystroke: **Alt+ 0233**. This means you can directly place that character into your document without going through the hassles of copying it. To access the code, hold down the Alt key and use the ten-key to enter the numeric digits.*

Clipboard Viewer

Clipbrd

Unlike other programs, the Clipboard is always on. It is like a little screen in the back of the computer. Its purpose is to act as a holder for data, being text and/or graphics. It is kind of like those little post-it notes. You can put information on the Clipboard and then use it later. Though the Clipboard is always active, it is not always visible. This is why Windows has a **Clipboard Viewer**. Its sole purpose is to show or view the contents of the Clipboard.

The Clipboard itself is a universal program. This means any other program can use it. In fact, any time you see an **edit** command like cut, copy or paste, it is the Clipboard which makes these commands possible.

In general, the **Clipboard Viewer** is a plain-looking window. Many times you will find it empty or maybe containing a few boring words. One way of utilizing the Clipboard Viewer is by using the **Print Screen key**. The Print Screen key is commonly found on most standard keyboards in the right hand corner. In the past, it was used to send "snap-shots" of the screen to a printer. This way you could print the contents of the screen with just one button. However, with the advent of complex graphics, this option is no longer possible, or is it?

With Windows, the Print Screen key now sends a "snap-shot" of the screen to the Clipboard, instead of the printer. Once in the Clipboard, that image can then be sent to a printer.

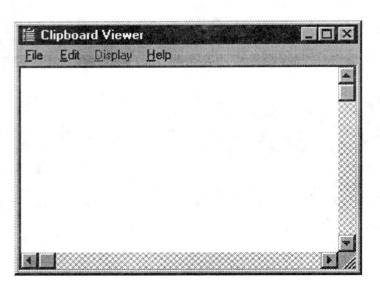

Figure 11.11
The Clipboard Viewer

HyperTerminal

Yikes, that's what I first thought when I saw this program. I freely admit, I avoided this program for months and I am sure many of my readers will do the same. However, the program itself is actually quite useful, especially in the age of the Internet. For many users this could be their ticket to the Information Super Highway.

HyperTerminal is a communication program. It allows you to connect with other systems or networks. It is a powerful program with well defined limits. It works only with text-based on-line services and cannot be used with graphic based bulletin boards, like the ones you might find on *America Online* or *Prodigy*. So, don't expect any fireworks when you use it, but mastering this program could give you access to the world.

In earlier versions of Windows, this program was called **Terminal** and it could only handle grabbing basic files. Its replacement, **HyperTerminal** is much more sophisticated. As for the Internet, Hyperterminal operates quite well with many independent access providers and can be used as a good first step towards getting connected. Using HyperTerminal is far easier than it may seem, here is how to get started.

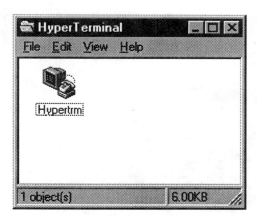

Figure 11.12
The Hyper-Terminal Program

In the window shown above, there is an icon associated for every connection established with another system. When you want to restore communication between that system, simply click on its icon. If this is your first time using HyperTerminal, there will be only one icon in the window.

To establish a new connection, double-click on the **Hypertrm** icon. At first, you will be asked is to **name** the connection and give it an **icon**. For us, a good name for our connection would be the *Internet*, since this is a good way to get access it through Windows. In actuality, you have to go through an access provider to gain complete entry to the Internet. But doing it this way will allow you to see the interaction in Windows instead of seeing it in DOS.

Figure 11.13
Naming the connection

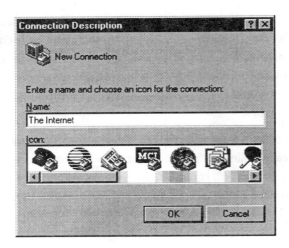

The next screen will ask you to enter the **phone number** of the system you are trying to contact. For the Internet, this would be the number of one of those independent companies.

Figure 11.14
Selecting a phone number

After obtaining a phone number, the modem will attempt to make a connection with that number. To initiate this procedure, you need to click on the **Dial** button.

Figure 11.15
Making a connection

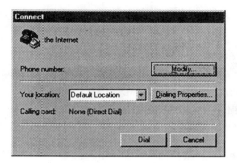

When the connection is made, the rest of the time is spent in the window shown below. This basic window has lots of standard features, including some speed buttons. The most important button is the **hang-up** button. It is used to end your session.

Figure 11.16
Connected with Hyper-Terminal

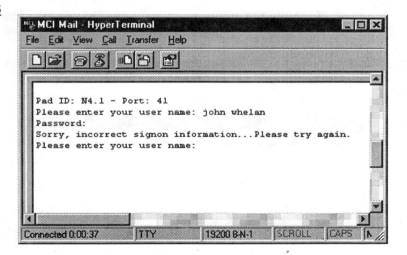

After completing the connection, an icon will be set up for it by HyperTerminal. So the next time, all you need to do is click on that icon to restore the connection.

Notepad

Notepad

The **Notepad** is another simple program which comes with Windows 95. It is a word processor designed for quick jobs. So, I don't recommend using it for making resumes.

Notepad is another of the programs left over from Windows 3.1 and in its hay day, Notepad was for some people, their only access to a word processor. But with Windows 95, you are given a better choice. You can use Notepad or Wordpad. Wordpad is a program which gets much closer to the concept of a word processor. I will examine it at the end of this chapter, but for now let's look at Notepad.

Notepad has few if any special features which may go completely unused. One of its big advantages, it is very fast. Mostly because, it can't do a whole lot. It can't store any special formatted characters and Notepad can't handle any type of graphics. It is basically a stripped down text editor.

Another advantage of the Notepad is its ability to keep track of time. No other program has this unique feature. It allows you to keep a journal or log on the computer. You can write entries and Notepad will keep track of the time they were entered. Here is how it works:

❶ Start with opening a new file. In this example, we will call our file the Captain's Log.

Figure 11.17
The Notepad, notice the location of the word **.LOG**

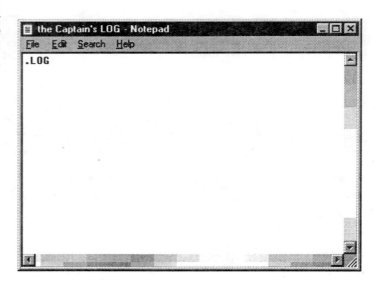

❷ The next step is to type the word LOG preceded by a period, like so **.LOG**, at the top left-hand corner of the window.

❸ After typing this sequence, you will want to save it. It is at this point where you can name the file as well, use the opportunity to be creative. I called my file the Captain's Log.

Now, every time you open this file (the Captain's Log, for example), you will see the time stamped at the beginning of each journal entry, as shown below. This way you can follow your entries just like a real journal. Windows 95 also sets up an icon for the file at the Start up screen with the other system icons, so it will be easy to access.

Figure 11.18
The Notepad (i.e. the Captain's Log)

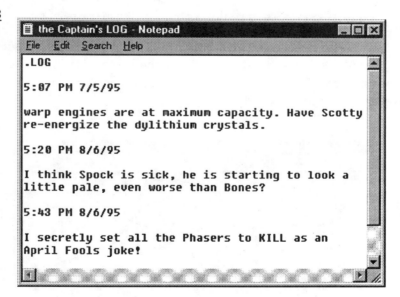

In addition, the time and date can be inserted manually at any point by simply pressing the **F5** key.

Notepad is well adapted for office use. It can handle lots of abuse while at the same time, need little or no maintenance. As a program, it is very secure and can be trusted with sensitive material. In addition, it can be set up in a networking environment, so everyone works from the same file. In general, Notepad is a lot like its physical ancestor, the notebook. Both are proficient and necessary in an informational society.

Paint

Paint is probably the most popular and one of the most used program in the Windows 95 accessories group. It is a favorite of both amateurs and professionals alike. It has a simple interface, yet possesses the ability to accomplish some pretty complex tasks.

Paint is basically a simple graphics program. It allows its users to create and manipulate computer graphics. It is the ability to create graphics which makes this program so unique. Despite popular belief, most graphic programs do not allow users to create a drawing from scratch.

In addition, you should not be fooled by this program's child-like appearance. It is a very powerful program as well. In fact, most of the graphics in this book were enhanced or modified by the Paint program in Windows 95.

Paint is essentially an improved version of **Paint Brush**, an old Windows 3.1 program. It continues the tradition of an uncomplicated layout mixed with a host of popular tools. Tools like spray cans, pencils, erasers and (of course) paint brushes; lets anyone's imagination go wild.

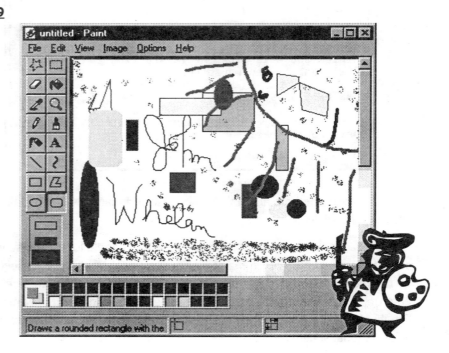

Figure 11.19
The Paint Program

However, working in Paint may not be as easy as it seems. For starters, the mouse is not a great tool for creating designs. It is very difficult to get the mouse to stay steady. You also have to fight with screen resolution and clarity. In the end, I believe even Van Gogh couldn't make a masterpiece from Paint, so do not expect your creations to even come close.

Paint also comes with several tools to help you create designs. These tools include many different types of brushes, magnifiers and shape manipulators. Most of them are pretty easy to understand and use. But, when it comes to colors, painting can be a little tricky.

Figure 11.20
The Color Palette

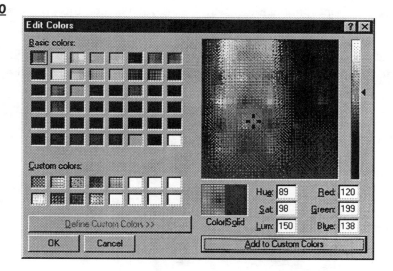

Paint gives you access to **28** different colors to start with. These are not real complex colors, just the basic ones. To make a particular color, double-click on one of the colors and then use the color palette, as shown above.

Generally, there are two places colors can be used; the **foreground** and the **background**. To add a color to the foreground click on the **left** mouse button. To add a color to the background click on the **right** mouse button.

Paint can also be used to design Wallpaper for the Windows 95 landscape. This way you can customize your screen and give it a real personal look. To do this, start with making a creation. However, instead of saving it, click on the **Set As Wallpaper (Center)** option. This will put your work of art on display so all your friends can see it.

Phone Dialer

The Phone Dialer is another really neat program which is included with Windows 95 and it has not been available to previous Windows users before. It only has one job, which is to make phone calls for you. It acts just like an electric phone and even keeps track of who you call. It is easy to use and helps make any computer into a one-stop secretary.

Phone Dialer

The Phone Dialer is found in the **Accessories** group and is a good program to get familiar with. You can add phone numbers to its speed dial buttons or use it as a conventional phone. Either way, I think you will find this program to be a noteworthy addition.

Assigning some numbers to the speed dial buttons is very easy. Start with clicking on the button you want to assign. I suggest working from the top down.

Figure 11.21
The Phone Dialer

When you click on the blank button, you are given a chance to put in a name and number. When entering the phone number remember <u>not</u> to include any hyphens. The Phone Dialer does not like them.

Figure 11.22
Entering names into the Phone Dialer

After entering the name and number, click on the **Save** button. This stores the phone number in memory and puts the name on one of the speed dial button.

Repeat these steps until you have filled up all the speed dial buttons. Now, if you want to call someone, simply click on the appropriate button and wait. After a few seconds, it will be safe to pick up the phone and have a chat.

One of the really neat features of the Phone Dialer is its **Phone Log**. This is a log which records all the phone calls you make while using the Phone Dialer. The log includes who you called, what time you called  and how long you were on the phone with them. This is a good way of monitoring your phone calls and may help you control your phone bill. The log can also be printed out, so you can keep a printed record of your phone calls. To see this log, click on **Show Log** in the **Tools** pull-down menu.

Deleting a name from the speed dial buttons can be a bit tricky, since every time you touch a button the Phone Dialer starts calling. The best way to delete one without getting too messy is by selecting **Speed Dial...** on the **Edit** pull down menu. Doing this allows the user to add and remove names from the speed dial buttons. Without this option, you would have to do some pretty mean things to remove some of those names (like re-installation).

When you find the name and number of the person you want to delete, simply replace their name and number with blank spaces. This will effectively delete them.

Figure 11.23
Removing a name and number

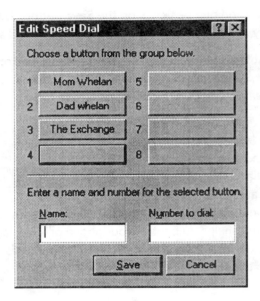

As I mentioned earlier in this chapter, the Phone Dialer can be used in conjunction with the **Cardfile** program. The Cardfile, you'll remember is a simplified address book. Both programs share a similar function, the ability to store names and numbers. So, if the Phone Dialer's speed buttons are not large enough to hold all your acquaintances, try checking out the Cardfile program. It has a lot more room.

THE TEN PACK

Wordpad

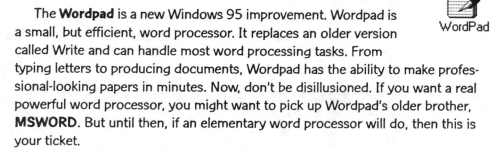
WordPad

The **Wordpad** is a new Windows 95 improvement. Wordpad is a small, but efficient, word processor. It replaces an older version called Write and can handle most word processing tasks. From typing letters to producing documents, Wordpad has the ability to make professional-looking papers in minutes. Now, don't be disillusioned. If you want a real powerful word processor, you might want to pick up Wordpad's older brother, **MSWORD**. But until then, if an elementary word processor will do, then this is your ticket.

Wordpad comes with all the necessities of a programmable typewriter. It can handle fonts of different shapes and sizes, as well as hold graphics. It has a standard editor with cut, copy and paste commands. It even has an "undo" button, to erase recent mistakes. Unfortunately, it does not have a spell checker, a thesaurus or a grammer checker.

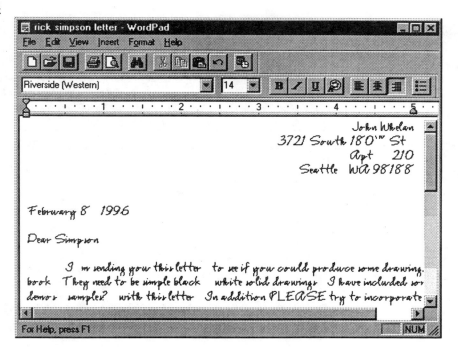

Figure 11.24
Wordpad, the Word Processor included in Windows 95

Wordpad is full of options which are basically the scaled down versions of the ones you might expect to find in a more expensive word processor. They include date/time stamps, bullet styles, fancy character alignments and the ability to add color. All of these options are accessible from the speed buttons, as pointed out below.

Figure 11.25
Using Wordpad

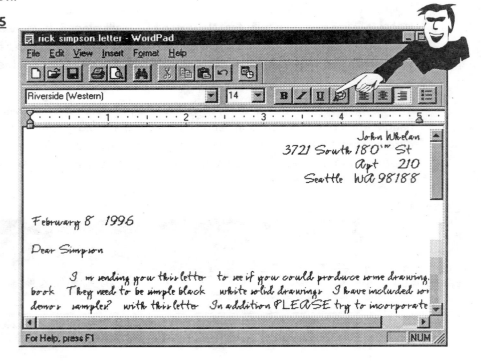

The Utilities

CHAPTER 12

Windows 95 comes with a host of utilities, all designed to take advantage of the operating system's new improvements and help monitor them. These programs provide a way of protecting valuable data, as well as insuring a computer's health. Microsoft's operating systems in the past have always included an assortment of safeguards, programs like Scandisk or MS Backup. However, with Windows 95, the number and power of these utilities has grown substantially. In this chapter, I examine all of these utilities and demonstrate the best ways to use them.

What is a Utility?

In the past, I use to describe Utilities as any programs which weren't games or business applications. They were basically the programs I could never understand. This is a rather naive way of thinking in today's market, but to a certain point, I think you will find that it does hold true.

Perhaps a better way of describing Utilities is to think of them as computer doctors. They work very well when a computer is sick and even do a better job at preventing system problems in the first place. Utilities themselves range in everything from memory managers to virus protectors. These types of programs can be purchased in any computer retail stores and can sometimes require a rather large degree of technical knowledge.

In addition, Windows 95 also comes with a few utilies of its own. Although it does not come with every utility in the book, it does come with quite a few important ones. All of which are quite easy to use and understand.

Microsoft Backup

MS Backup is the first utility I will explore. Like the name implies, it is used to make backup copies for files. Backup copies are duplicates of the original files, which are used when the originals are damaged. These backup copies are saved on disk and then should be stored in a safe place; so, if something does go wrong in the future, you will be prepared. Think of it as buying insurance. Making backups will cost you only time and the price of a few blank diskettes, the alternative could end up costing you a lot more.

MS Backup is an inviting program. Its layout is designed not to intimidate users, but rather encourage them. Microsoft knows the importance of this program and wanted to make sure its users wouldn't be afraid of it. The only human analogy I can think of, is comparing it to going to the dentist.

To use MS Backup, start by clicking on the Backup icon, it is located with all the other Windows 95 utilities, just beyond the **Accessories** directory in the **System Tools** folder.

Figure 12.1
MS Backup's Introduction window

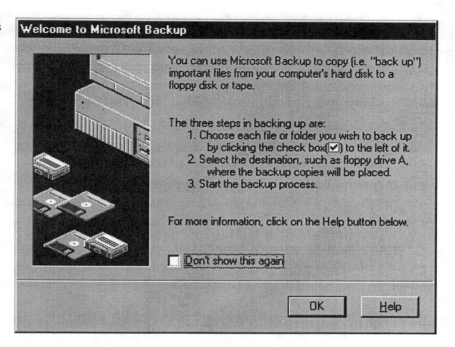

The first window appears after starting the program and provides you with the basic instructions. It consists of **three** steps which include:

① **Identify** the files to backup
② **Select** a backup drive
③ **Start** backing up the files

If this makes sense to you, then you can start the process by clicking on the **OK** button. But if these instructions are a little too brief for such an important task, let me take this opportunity to expand a little more.

First, when selecting the files to back up, it is important to consider which files to copy. Windows 95 not only allows you to make backup copies of itself, but of other programs, as well. You are only limited by the number of blank diskettes you have and the amount of time you are willing to spend. Since this process does take a fair amount of time and diskettes, I strongly recommend only backing up important files; like Windows 95, DOS or books you may currently be writing.

Figure 12.2
Selecting the files to backup

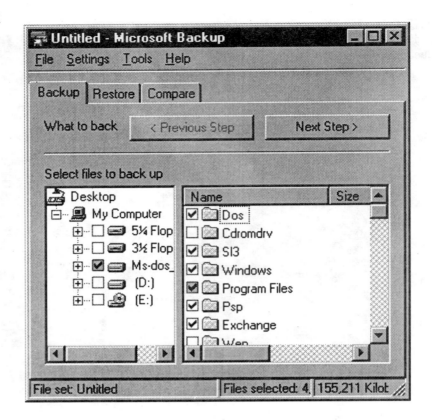

In the window shown above, you can select individual files, as well as entire directories. As you choose files to backup, MS Backup starts to prepare them. This process takes a little time, although this is really only a small percentage of the time you will spend. The majority of the time is spent copying.

The next step is to select a destination drive. This is the drive where the backups are copied to. In most cases, the choice will already be made for you, since there are not many computers around with multiple disk drives.

However, if you own a tape drive, Windows 95 will automatically detect it. A tape drive is a much more efficient way to backup a system, because a single tape can hold up 100 times more data than a disk could.

Figure 12.3
Selecting a destination drive

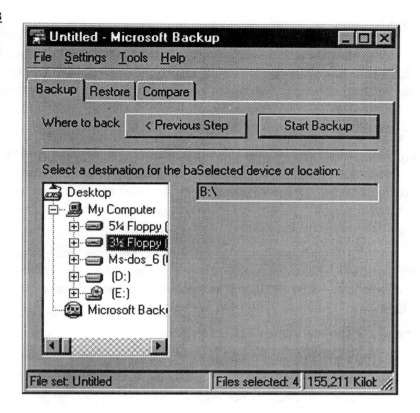

The final step in the process is to copy the files, by clicking on the **Start Backup** button. MS Backup will prompt you when it is time to exchange diskettes and will also provide a chart showing the percentage of files left to copy.

Making backup copies is a real "live and learn" experience. An experience better off not experiencing, for those people who think system problems do not exist. Subsequently, system problems and their consequences are very real. They may be caused by such minor events as power outages or the build up of dust. Other problems could result from computer viruses. These viruses are spread from computer to computer much like its human analogy. The accumulation of uncommon and unnoticed files, too could bring a system down. In the end, a computer system is a lot like any natural environment. It is extremely fragile where every individual component depends upon each other. MS Backup is just one part in a long line of defenses designed to help protect your computer and its data from any potential problems.

Scandisk

Scandisk is a program which has been in the Microsoft family since the early DOS years. Its basic function is to check the hard drive for any abnormalities and correct them. Scandisk does this in two ways: first it checks the files on the hard drive, then it physically scans the surface of the hard drive to find any errors.

Scandisk is <u>not</u> a virus-detecting program, it's only designed to identify disk problems. These kind of problems occur when certain files are used exceedingly and then cause discrepancies with the systems' past behavior. These files usually go unnoticed by average Windows users. However, eventually the build up of them can cause system problems. So to avoid any of these problems, users should run Scandisk at least once a month.

Scandisk is completely independent from its predecessors, meaning it can find problems unique to Windows 95, which other disk scanners couldn't locate. You can start Scandisk by clicking on its icon, which is located in the same directory as MS Backup.

Figure 12.4
Scandisk

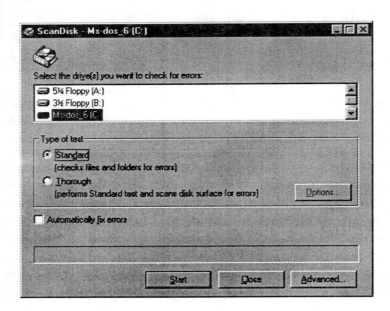

As soon as you decide which drive to scan, the program is ready to go. Scandisk doesn't really need any further instructions. The process begins after you click the **Start** button and is over in a few minutes.

The Utilites

The time Scandisk takes to scan a drive is heavily dependent upon the size of the drive and how many files are on it. A large hard drive with lots of files on it could take a rather long time, whereas a smaller drive with less files may only take seconds.

Upon the completion of the scan, you are given the scan results. In most cases, these results are rather boring and uninteresting. However, pay close attention to the **bad sectors**. If any appear, you may want to acquire some help.

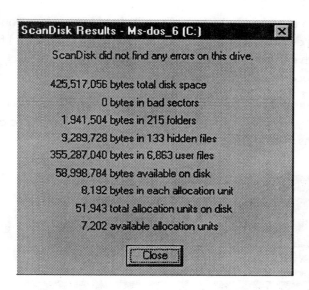

Figure 12.5
The results of Scandisk

Scandisk not only finds problems, but it fixes them as well. Since most of these problems are highly systemmatic, you are much better off allowing Windows to fix them.

You can also choose to scan the surface of a disk, by clicking on the **Thorough** button. This process takes longer, because the physical surface of most drives is rather large. Subsequently, surface scans do not have to be performed as often as file scans.

Surface problems are caused by very small particles. Since the average head on a disk drive is no larger than a single thread of hair, almost any fragment could cause damage to the drive. Materials like chalk dust and sea breeze pose real threats to hard drives. Though most household computers operate in fairly safe conditions, it is still a good idea to surface scan a drive every couple of months.

Compressing Data

Compressing data basically allows you to get more bang for your buck. All users are limited by the physical amount of space they have on their hard drives. The idea behind data compression is to allow users the ability to utilize the maximum amount of space. Thus turning a wimpy drive into a warehouse. The program which does this is called **DriveSpace** and its also located in the **System Tools** folder with the other Windows 95 utilities.

Does this seem too good to be true? Then it shouldn't surprise you to find out data compression does have its drawbacks. For starters, Compressed files may not be compatible with certain programs. Another disadvantage is the lack of performance you may receive with some compressed files.

On the other hand, DriveSpace can be used to free up **50** to **100** percent more space. This is a very significant amount of space and has the ability to cause users to rethink any plans of upgrading their hard drives.

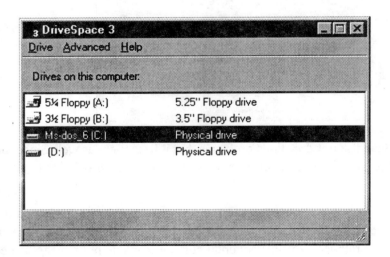

Figure 12.6
DriveSpace

DriveSpace lets you compress floppy diskettes as well as hard drives. However, it doesn't allow you to select a CD-ROM drive, because the data on a CD-ROM's is <u>read only</u> and CD-ROMs do not permit any writing or changing of the data on them.

After choosing a drive to compress, click on the **Compress...** option which is located in the pull down menu under the **Drive** selection.

The Utilites

Figure 12.7
Compressing a drive

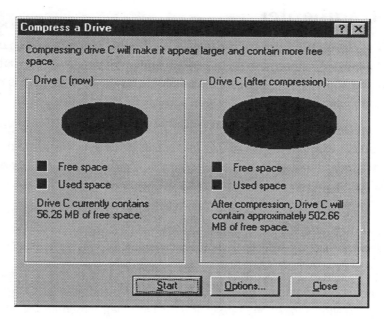

The window shown above, displays the results of the data compression, even before the actual compression ever transpires. This way you can see the space you're gaining and, if you like what you see, push the **Start** button. Data compression does take awhile, heavily depending upon the size of the drive or disk being compressed; so be patient.

Disk Defragmenter

Disk Defragmenter is seldom used. Exactly what it does could be considered a bit of a mystery. It has nothing to do with computer viruses or corrupt files. The Defragmenter is designed to make computers run better and, here is what is understood about it:

> When a system writes out to a file, it puts the data anywhere it wants to on the hard drive. This means two pieces of data for the same program could be located on opposite ends of the hard drive, thus causing the computer not to run as smoothly as it could.
>
> Now, the Disk Defragmenter's job is to put all randomly spread data into their correct spots. By putting similar data close to each other, a computer will not have to work as hard.

These improvements may go completely unnoticed or may make a significant difference, depending on the size of the hard drive and how badly the data may have been allocated. At any rate, using the Disk Defragmenter will not cause any harm and may fix a disk irregularity which otherwise could have been difficult to diagnose.

Like the other Windows 95 utilities, the Disk Defragmenter is located past the **Accessories** directory in the **System Tools** folder. This program does not take a lot of input to get it going. Just select the drive and click the **OK** button.

Figure 12.8
Selecting the drive to Defragment

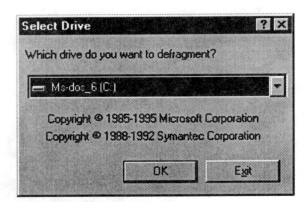

The whole process could take a couple of minutes or even an hour, again depending heavily on the size of the hard drive. While it's processing the Defragmenter provides a chart showing the percentage of tracks it has left.

Figure 12.9
Defragmenting a Hard Drive

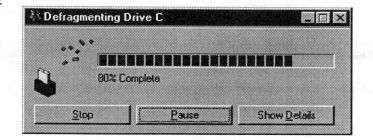

Unlike Scandisk, Defragmenting is not something which is done on a timely basis. A drive could need attention twice in one day, or may go untouched for weeks. The only one who knows when a drive needs to be defragmented is Windows. Subsesquently, if a drive doesn't need to be defragmented, Windows will tell you!

Figure 12.10
A drive, where the defragmenter is not needed

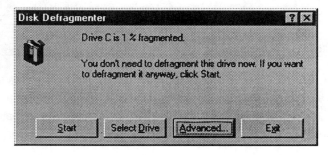

System Monitor

The System Monitor is a unique tool. Unlike the other utilities, it doesn't really do anything. It can't fix or diagnosis any problems. All it does is sit and watch the computer work. (What a job!)

Figure 12.11
The System Monitor

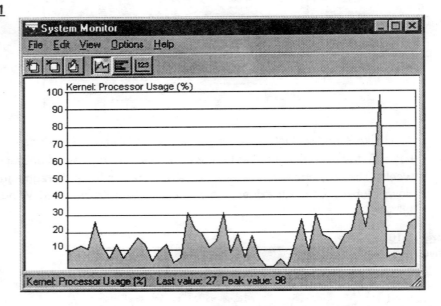

The System Monitor tracks processor usage. This essentially tells us how hard a computer is working. In the window shown above, the graph displays the percentage of how much of the CPU is being used. As more programs are activited, the percentage rises.

There are a few adjustments which can be made to the System Monitor. For starters, the time interval can be increased to a second by second pace. This can be done in the **Options** selection on the menu bar. In addition, the appearance of the window can be altered, by selecting a different **View** option.

If you **Hide the title bar** on the System Monitor, the best way to get it back is by pressing the **Esc** key.

The Games

CHAPTER 13

Windows 95 wouldn't be complete without some computer games. So, Microsoft has included four of them with its operating system. They are not meant to put Nintendo out of business, but after a few tests, I am sure you will see how addicting these games can be. The games include **Solitaire**, **Minesweeper**, **Hearts** and **FreeCell**. All these games come standard with Windows 95 and are located in the **Accessories** directory. In this chapter, I showcase each game as well as provide some useful hints.

Solitaire

Solitaire has always been a part of the Windows family. Solitaire involves the combination of luck and skill, which makes it challenging, as well as addicting.

The Windows version of Solitaire is played like the real life card game, except the computer does all the dealing. In addition, it also keeps count of your score and keeps all the cards in order. Here is how the game is played. Start by clicking on the **Solitaire** icon. It is located within the **Games** folder (just past the **Accessories** directory).

Figure 13.1
The Game of Solitaire

The main idea behind Solitaire is to get rid of all the cards on the screen. You do this by dragging them into the four card slots in the right hand corner of the screen. What makes the game difficult is the cards have to be placed sequentially, starting with the Ace and ending with the King. They also must alternate in colors.

The game starts when you click on the deck of cards at the top left hand corner. After that, every card is at your disposal to help you clear the screen. Use them to stack cards and move other cards out of the way.

The game ends when you run out of options while not clearing all the cards from the screen, in which case you lose; or if all the cards have been placed in the top slots, in which case you win.

If you are dealt a card which belongs in the right hand corner, like an ace, just *double click* on that card and the computer will automatically place the card in the correct spot. The computer also will not allow you to put a card in the wrong spot. Much like any card game, it is often better off to play the game a couple of times to get the hang of it, instead of reading some instructions on how to play. In any case, if you have ever played a game of Solitaire when you were young or just lonely, you should be able to pick up the game very quickly and in no time, master it. Solitaire, like all the Windows games, makes a great time killer.

Figure 13.2
A game of Solitaire in progress

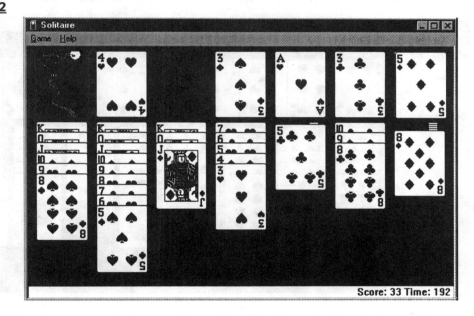

After playing the game for awhile, try exploring some of the **Game** options. You can change the way the game is played and even the color of the cards. When you have finished playing, just close the Solitaire window and the game will be stopped. Then, if you want to play again, the game will restart with a fresh new deck of cards.

Solitaire was available in previous versions of Windows and has long been a computer junkie's favorite. For a long time it was the only card game which was included with Windows. However, with Windows 95, two more additional card games have been added. They are the game of **Hearts** and **FreeCell**.

FreeCell

FreeCell is a card game which Windows NT users have seen before. It was included in the Windows NT package and did not receive as much attention as Solitaire. However, it has been given another chance and was included with Windows 95.

At first, FreeCell may look a lot like Solitaire. However, it is played a lot differently. For starters, you are dealt the entire deck at the beginning of the game. Then instead of dragging cards, you click them into their correct locations.

Figure 13.3
The Game of FreeCell

The main idea of this game is to sort the cards in order by suit, and then number them from the Ace to the King on the four right hand slots. While moving the cards, you can use the left-hand slots as temporary holding spots. You win if you can complete all four slots in the right-hand corner. Otherwise, you lose.

FreeCell actually comes with **32,000** different games, all consisting of different initial card arrangements. Each game does have a possible solution. However, finding some of these solutions can prove to be very difficult. If you do start a game which seems too difficult, just start over and pick a different card arrangement. Also, remember to take time to explore FreeCell's **Game** options.

During your playing career, FreeCell keeps track of your wins and losses. This way you can chart your progress. This statistics are reset after exiting the game.

Figure 13.4
FreeCell statistics

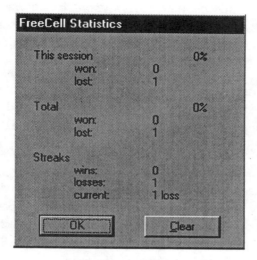

FreeCell isn't as addicting as some of the other Windows games and can become very frustrating at times. It also lacks character and physical appeal. Because, when you think about it, most cards games need either surprises or wagers to make them exciting, FreeCell comes with neither.

Hearts

Hearts is another card game which is included with Windows 95. The game first showed up on computer in *Windows for Workgroups*. Hearts was one of the first card games which took advantage of today's network setup. Presently, with Windows 95, this allows users to play against the computer or with other neighbors.

Hearts is played on the computer in the same way as it is played in real life. A person puts a card onto the table and everyone else puts down a card of the same suit. Then, the person placing the highest card in the pile takes all the cards. If you do not possess the suit of the card which is put down, you can then play any other card you want.

To win the game, you need to obtain the **lowest score**. Any card with a heart is worth one point, hence how the game got its name. The Queen of Spades is worth 13 points. However, if one of the players is able to acquire all the hearts and the Queen of Spades, then that player doesn't get any points and all the other players are penalized 26 points. This is known as *shooting the moon*.

The game starts by asking your name. If you are alone, the computer will control the other players, because the game of Hearts is usually played with **four** people.

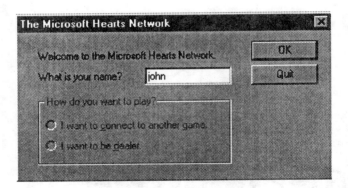

Figure 13.5
Starting the Game of Hearts

After obtaining your name, the game is ready to go. As in the real life version, the first move you do is pass off **three** cards to your neighbor. During this initial move, you will want to discard the worst cards in your hand. These frequently include any high Hearts, Aces or high Spades.

Figure 13.6
The Game of Hearts in Progress

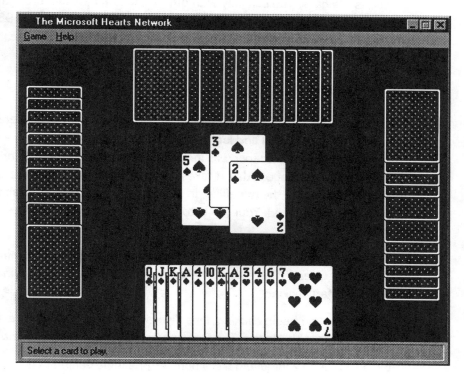

As the game proceeds, all the players put in their cards and the highest card then takes the pile. During the game, Hearts actually tells you what to do, by leaving instructions at the bottom **left hand** corner of the window.

Keep in mind, Hearts is a game of points, unlike Solitaire. You want to retain the lowest score following each game. Then a Score Sheet is displayed periodically at the end of each game and it displays the players in order of their score. Remember, a high score is bad.

Figure 13.7
The Score Sheet in Hearts

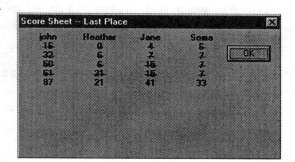

Hearts is a game you can play with others and is accessible through internal networks. It is the last of the card games to be included in Windows 95. The only other game remaining in Windows 95 isn't a card game, but a game called Minesweeper.

Minesweeper

Minesweeper is my personal favorite Windows game. It is a challenging game requiring both logical skill and luck. It, like Solitaire, has always been a part of the Windows family. Minesweeper was included in earlier versions of Windows and is still a part of the package today. It takes its name from the goal of the game; to detect all the mines in the minefield. In this game, a mine is a bomb and if you click on one you're dead. Your job is to flag all the mines, so people won't click on them.

So, how do you detect mines in the first place? Well at the beginning there is only one way. Guess? That's right, the best way to start a game of Minesweeper is to randomly start clicking.

But, before you begin clicking, let's discuss the game a little more. Minesweeper has three skill levels. The first one being the easiest and so on.

Each square on a minefield has a number or a mine behind it. If the square has a number, then the number represents the number of mines surrounding that particular square. So, a square with the number **8** on it would be completely surrounded by mines. Now, once when a mine is detected, you must then flag it by clicking on it with the right-hand mouse button.

Use logic to detect each mine. If a square has the number **1** on it and is only surrounded by one other uncovered square. Then that square has to be a mine. Any squares which do not contain numbers or mines are just empty. This is because there are no mines close by, which is nothing to be alarmed about. If by chance you hit a mine, just click on the smile and a new game will be produced.

To win the game you have to detect all the mines. The number at the top left hand corner counts the number of mines left. Once you get the hang of it, Minesweeper can be really addicting.

Figure 13.8
The Game of Minesweeper in expert mode

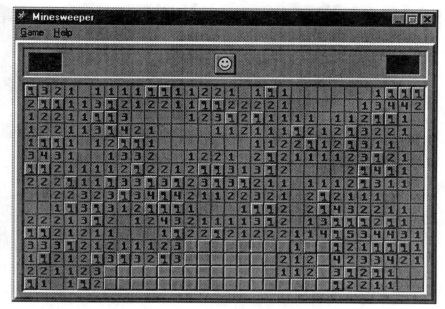

Minesweeper may look uninviting at first, but the game is really a lot of fun and very challenging. For starters, I recommend using the **Beginner** or **Intermediate** levels. Because they are doable. As you progress, you may want to custom design the size of the mine field by using the **Custom...** option.

The score in Minesweeper is based on the time it takes you to uncover all the mines. A low time produces a high score. This makes the game more challenging, since fast moves often lead to mistakes, especially when you are handling bombs!

Figure 13.9
A high score

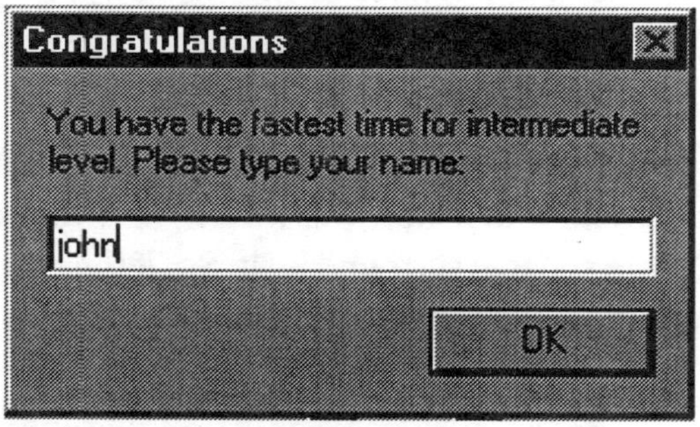

Top Secret Minesweeper Hints

Since I am very experienced at playing Minesweeper, I'll use this opportunity to pass on some of my Top Secrets Minesweeper hints. These secrets have been tested and proven effective. Furthermore, these secrets should not be openly discussed among Windows users. Please read each secret carefully and then proceed to use them. They should improve your success at finding mines!

① Whenever a square is showing a **3** and there are only three uncovered squares around it, then these squares <u>must</u> be mines. I know this seems obvious, but you would be surprised how many times people miss it.

② When a square is uncovered showing a **2** and it is surrounded by **1**s on both sides. Then, there has to be two mines located right beside the squares displaying the ones. This is a logical conclusion, because, if the mines were any place else, the numbers displayed on these squares would have to be different.

③ When a square is showing a **2** and it is following by another square showing a **2** and then followed by a square showing a **1**, the square directly beside the first **2** has to be a mine. This has to be the case, since there cannot be two mines by a square with a **1** on it.

④ My next secret works when you uncover a row of **1**s. The squares underneath (or above) them will alternate with mines. This means, for every safe square, there are two other unsafe squares surrounding it. So, if the row of squares are against a wall, it is safe to skip two squares and then click on the next one. As shown here:

⑤ This secret, I like to call the dead end. It starts when a square is uncovered with a **1** on it. This square is discovered just below another square which has a **1** on it. All the surrounding squares are untouched, as shown on the right.

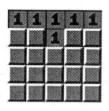

If the next square below the previously discovered one, has a **1** on it as well, then it is safe to click on all the surrounding squares. This is demostrated below. The reason this works, is that we know one of the two squares underneath the initial 1 has to be a mine!

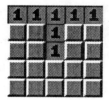 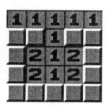

In general, most of my Top Secrets Minesweeper Hints are difficult to describe on paper. They each use logical deduction to conclude which square is safe to click on, or where a mine is. They usually pave the way for more free space while buying valuable time, especially when options are running low. In addition, with these hints, you can derive other ones and soon you will be a Minesweeper expert too.

Minesweeper is a unique game which requires unique skills. It can provide hours of anticipation and not to mention lots of fun.

Multimedia

CHAPTER 14

What is multimedia? Multimedia is a term which frequently accompanies most CD-ROM drives. In general, it means the mixing of two or more mediums, usually combining sounds and pictures. This is most apparent in multimedia software, where combinations of sounds, pictures and videos are often used to explore a topic. Because of its popularity, multimedia has its own section in Windows 95. It is located within the **Accessories** directory. The section has a total of four programs in it, three of which consist of some type of media playing software. While the fourth program is solely dedicated to controlling the overall volume.

Windows 95 comes with its own built-in multimedia package, which includes a Media Player, a Sound Recorder and a CD Player. It is the addition of the CD Player which really makes this package complete. Although most CD-ROM drives themselves automatically include some type of music software, Microsoft decided on making the CD Player a standard part of Windows 95, regardless if you already own one or not.

The CD Player

CD-ROM drives on most computers can handle programs as well as audio CDs, as long as the correct software is present. Luckily, this software is provided by Windows 95 in a program known as the CD Player.

The CD Player is located within the **multimedia** section. It is easy to use and someday may replace your entire home stereo. The player operates much like the ones found in the home electronics department of Sears, with most of its features coinciding with today's domestic CD players.

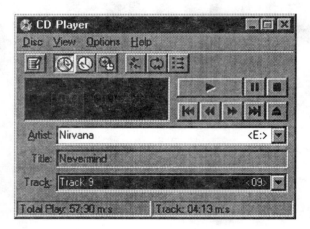

Figure 14.1
The CD Player

The buttons and the display on the CD player are exactly the same as its home version and should be inherently easy to interpret.

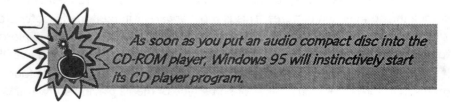

As soon as you put an audio compact disc into the CD-ROM player, Windows 95 will instinctively start its CD player program.

The CD Player has all the comforts of any Boom-box, although it isn't very portable, but given the right attention, it will ROCK! The table below outlines some of these comforts and explains what they do.

CD Player function	What it does
Random Track Order	Plays selections from the Compact disc in random order.
Continuous Play	Allows the CD Player to continuously; after reaching the last selection, it starts over.
Intro Play	Plays the first ten seconds of each selection on the disc. The number of seconds played can be adjusted.

The functions in the table above, are the same kind of functions you would expect to find on any home stereo system. They include all the popular audio necessities. Any of these functions can be chosen from the **Options** segment of the menu bar, as shown below:

Figure 14.2
The Options in the CD Player

The digital display on the CD Player can be adjusted, by clicking on it. Initially, it shows the track number with the elapsed time. However, after one click, it shows the time remaining on the track and after two clicks, it shows the time remaining on the disc.

The series of buttons on the face of the CD Player are shortcuts and are used to achieve the same functions I previously described above. The first set of buttons control the display while the second set work with the track selections.

Controlling the Volume

The volume of the CD Player is also able to control the volume of the entire system. It invokes a program called **Volume Control** and is accessible in three ways, as shown below.

① In the **View** option on the menu bar of the CD Player.

Figure 14.3
The View Option in the CD Player

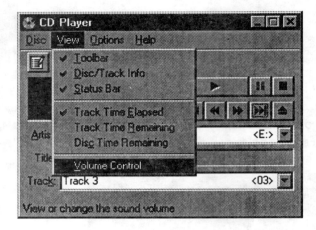

② From the start-up menu in the **Accessories** directory, within the **Multimedia** folder.

Figure 14.4
The Multimedia folder

③ By clicking or double-clicking on the speaker in the Taskbar. Clicking once activates the main volume switch, which only controls the general volume of the computer. However, clicking twice on the speaker in the Taskbar activates the **Volume Control** program.

Once the Volume Control program has been initiated, you have the ability to control the amplification of every component of the system, this includes Wave files, external accessories (like musical keyboards) and the CD Player, itself. The Volume Control is quite simple to operate and is completely mouse driven.

Figure 14.5
The Volume Control program

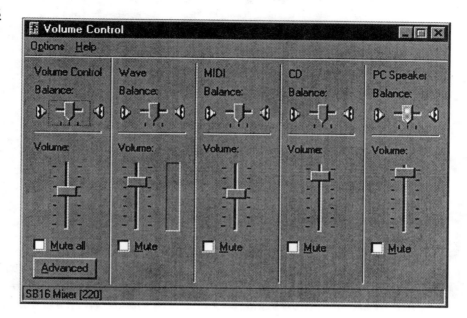

The Volume Control is separated into divisions, much like a professional mixing board. These divisions represent different audio components of a system. For example, the PC speakers occupy a division within the display.

Even though the Volume Control has the capability of showing a huge range of components, it is not always necessary to have all of them showing at once. For instance, you may not own any PC speakers, so there is no point in having the volume control of them visible. Fortunately, the Volume Control allows us to accommodate its display to show only the components we want.

To take advantage of this option, you need to open the **Properties** window, which is found in the **Options** segment of the pull down menu. In this window, you can select the components you want to display on the Volume Control, simply by clicking on them, as shown on the next page.

Figure 14.6
The Properties window of the Volume Control

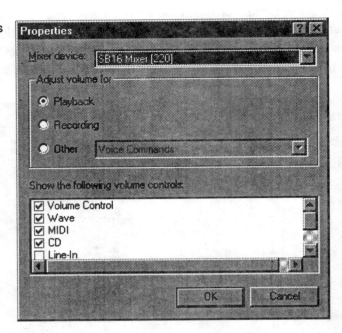

Some of the words in the window shown above, may seem a little foreign to some readers, since computer/audio terminology is seldom interpreted. Let me start by explaining how Windows works with sounds. When a sound is stored on a computer, it has to be represented by some sort of file. How the sound is produced usually determines what kind of file it will be stored in.

There are many kinds of file formats for sounds. Each format is suited to a particular medium. For example, in Windows, the most common file format for a sound is a wave file (**.WAV**). Wave files make up almost all the sounds you hear in windows (all those beeps and gongs). While MIDI files (**.MID**) are produced from external devices, such as an electronic keyboard. There are also voice files (**.VOC**) to account for human voices.

In order to use some of these formats, you must possess the medium which produces them (*like an electronic keyboard for MIDI files*). Subsequently, if you do not own any of these devices, it is not necessary to show the volume switch related to that format.

The Volume Control is not the only thing you can customize in Windows 95, the music itself can be adjusted to accommodate users taste, as well.

Customizing CDs

One advantage this player has over domestic CD players is the ability to customize the CDs it uses. The CD Player in Windows 95 lets you name the disc and its selections. Then it remembers the names and your favorite selections every time the disc is played. This is all done for you automatically.

You can program your favorite songs into the computer, so they are played and saved. For this type of customizing, follow these simple steps.

❶ Start by clicking on the **Disc** option in the menu bar, as shown below.

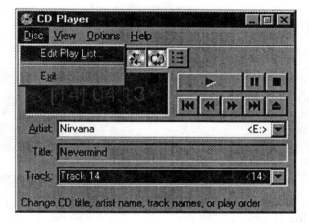

Figure 14.7
Customizing CDs

❷ From here select the **Edit Play List...**.

❸ This will open the **Disc Settings** window. In this window, you will find spots to place the name of the artist (or group), the title of the album and the title of each individual song. But, the main purpose of this window is to program the selections which you want to hear. Upon doing so, the selections will be automatically saved for future use. This way you can listen to what you want, when you want. *(continued on the next page)*

Figure 14.8
Programming the Disc Selections

- To program the selections you want to listen to, begin by clearing the list, by clicking on the **Clear All** button. Then proceed to choose a title from the **Available Tracks:** list. As the selection is highlighted, click on the **<Add** button, so the song is added to the **Play List**. Continue this routine until the Play List consists of all the selections you want to hear.

- This window also lets you rename all the selections so they correspond to the names on the CD cover. After a few minutes, your computer will look a lot like a professional DJ booth and may even start to sound like one.

Customizing the CD Player

After making your own customized CDs, you might feel the urge to do the same thing to your CD Player. You can customize the CD Player in two ways.

The **first** way of customizing the CD Player deals with most of the non-technical material and is pretty simple to understand. Unfortunately the alterations are simple, too, and may go completely unnoticed by everyone except yourself. These adjustment can be made by selecting the **Preferences...** segment in the **Options** pull down menu. This will open the Preferences window and allow you to make some minor system changes, as shown below.

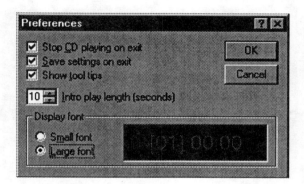

Figure 14.9
The CD Player's Preferences window

Most of the choices in the CD Player's Preferences window are of minor importance. They just refer to simple things which seem to have been left out or forgotten, when first originally designed.

The **second** way of customizing the CD player is in the **Multimedia Properties** window of the Control Panel. This window is much more technical and completely surpasses the CD player's own properties. It is like going to your Boss' Boss.

To view it, you need to go to the **Control Panel** and find the **Multimedia** icon. This icon is in charge of all the audio/video output in a computer, assuming you own a CD-ROM or a sound card. Don't confuse the Multimedia icon with the Sounds icon. They are two completely different programs.

In the Control Panel, the Sounds icon is mainly responsible for smaller sounds generated by Windows itself, whereas the Multimedia icon is mainly responsible for sounds generated from outside of Windows; like music. Both icons are also discussed in Chapter 7, entitled The Control Panel.

Clicking on the **Multimedia** icon from the Control Panel, opens the Multimedia Preferences window. From here, you can adjust the volume or change the parameters, on any audio device; by selecting that device and making the appropriate changes.

As for any specifications you might encounter, I strongly suggest consulting the makers of the particular devices before making any drastic changes. Because the multimedia package in Windows 95 is tied to the entire system and the changes you make here will, effect more than just the music of CDs.

Figure 14.10
The Multimedia Properties window

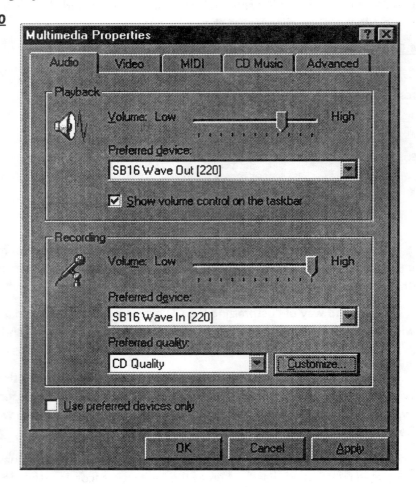

Using the Media Player and Sound Recorder

Windows 3.1 had a Media Player and a Sound Recorder. In fact, the Media Player was often used to play audio CDs when necessary. However, the CD Player within Windows 95 is much more efficient and useful than the Media Player at playing audio CDs. Yet, in desperate cases, the Media Player can do a suitable job.

Figure 14.11
The Media Player, playing Audio CDs

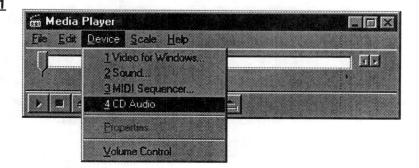

Like the name implies, the **Media Player** can only play sound or video files. It is what is commonly known as a multimedia device.

As you will remember, multimedia is the mixing of two or more mediums, usually combining sounds and pictures. Consequently, this allows media players to play videos. Actually, this is their primary function. However, inorder to do this, the video must be in a special format. An **.AVI** format, which stands for **A**udio **V**ideo **I**nput, is the only format the Media Player can recognize for videos. Luckily for us, Most videos are already stored on a computer in this format.

As for recording, that task is left to another device known as the **Sound Recorder**. The Sound Recorder is used to store sounds on a computer. Depending on what input devices you own, you can record everything from your favorite Windows sounds to your own voice. But, be warned, recording takes up a lot of disk space, so take it easy!

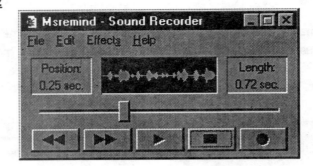

Figure 14.12
The Sound Recorder

The Sound Recorder only works with one type of file, **Waves files**. Any sound produced by a program in Windows, is generated through a Wave file. They are files which end with a **.WAV** extension. Unfortunately, audio CDs do not produce Wave files and cannot play on a Sound Recorder.

In order to record audio CDs, you have to convert the CD file into a Wave file through another means. Windows 95 does not include such a program, although most Sound Cards, CD-ROMs or Multimedia packages do.

Sending and Receiving Faxes

CHAPTER 15

A fax machine is simply a telephone which instead of carrying voices, sends data. Since data is the package it delivers, there is no need for a fax machine to be an external device. Today, fax machines can be well hidden inside a computer and still serve as well as they did when first introduced. Windows 95 comes with its own built-in fax machine and it is probably the only one you will ever need. It has the ability to send and receive faxes as well as create cover letters. This unique combination of features is thoroughly discussed throughout this chapter.

What is a fax?

Fax machines were invented as means of transferring data. The name **fax** comes from the word facsimile, which means to copy. Copying is the fundamental function of a fax machine. After producing a copy of a document, a fax machine then is able to transmit that copy through phone lines to another fax machine. Some fax machines actually double as copiers.

In this age of technology, yesterday's fax machines are now able to fit inside of personal computers. This means, you can have all the comforts of a fax machine, with only a few of the hassles. You can send or receive faxes, and not have to worry about where to store them, since everything is processed within the computer.

Unfortunately, the fax machines in today's computers don't always measure up to their predecessors. For starters, you can only send and receive documents from a computer. This means, everything you fax must first be in a computer to start with. This makes faxing pictures, photos and hand written papers almost impossible. In addition, like the fax machine you might find in someone's office, in order to receive a fax, a computer must be on and its phone line must be open.

Figure 15.1
A Fax Machine

What is a modem?

Before you can begin faxing, you have to know about modems. Modems are to faxing, like wheels are to cars. A modem is a necessary piece of hardware which is used to connect systems to other systems. In non-technical terms, a modem is a computer phone. Modems come in all shapes and sizes, but are basically divided into two categories:

① **External modems**

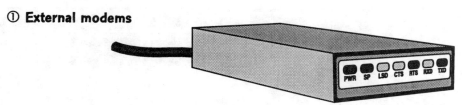

External modems, like their name implies, reside outside of a computer. They range in size, from a large shoe box to the smaller dimensions of a portable Walkman. Their front (or faces) all share the same characteristic lights, which flash in and out of sequence. External modems are more industrial and are used in places where abuse is common. As for the domestic user, an exterior modem may be a good option when all the space inside their computer has been filled up. Since the lights on a modem can provide important information, especially for trouble shooting, these modems may also be a popular choice for any control freaks.

② **Internal modems**

On the other hand, internal modems, are located primarily within a computer. Far from the sight of the average user, the only hint of their existence is usually the pair of their cable jacks found at the rear of a computer. Internal modems are often pre-installed within a computer and sold before a customer can even see what one physically looks like. So, if this kind of modem sounds foreign to you, chances are you may have an internal modem residing inside your computer.

Whether a modem is external or internal, it still does the same thing. They both transmit and receive data.

How modems transmit data is another feature which makes them different. Modems can transmit at different speeds and in different ways, by using data compression. The table below should help you get a better idea of how the different speeds of modems are divided up.

Speed of Modem	Description
1200 bps	1200 bits per second, considered to be very slow
2400 bps	2400 bits per second, slow, although this speed is very common in busy uses
9600 bps	9600 bits per second, still considered to be a slow modem
14,400 bps	14,400 bits per second, currently considered the industry standard
28,800 bps	28,800 bits per second, considered to be a fast modem

The speed at which data is transferred depends upon the speed of the two connected modems. Between the two modems, the modem with the slowest speed determines the speed of the data. For example, if you had a fast modem and it was sending data to a slower modem, the data would be transferred at a slower rate, even though you possessed a quick modem. In addition, modems are mainly priced by their speed.

A modem is the only actual requirement needed for sending and receiving faxes in Windows 95. As you may also encounter, many modems come with their own faxing software, which could make Microsoft's faxing program seem worthless.

However, compared with other communication programs, Microsoft's design is far simpler and much easier to use. It provides you with all the necessary features with none of the additional costs. Now, with all of this behind us, lets start sending some faxes.

Creating a Cover Page

What would a fax be without a cover page? In most cases, it would be lost. A cover page is very important in today's society. It provides people with valuable information which otherwise might have been wrongly assumed.

What is a cover page? A cover page is usually the first page which is faxed. It furnishes the recipient of the fax with essential information about the fax, he/she is receiving. The kind of information a cover page generally possesses varies quite a bit; but names, fax numbers and subject matter are very common.

To create a cover letter in Windows 95, you need to start with opening the **Cover Page Editor**. This program is found in the **Accessories** directory under the **Fax** folder. It is in this folder where all the faxing takes place.

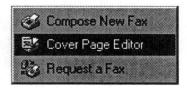

Figure 15.2
Using the Cover Page Editor

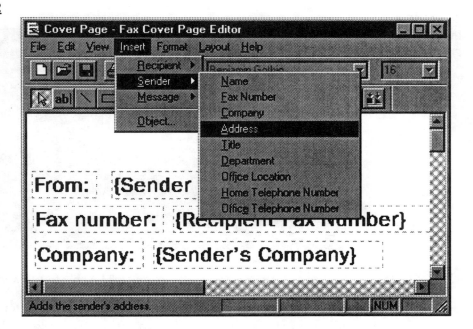

Once inside the cover page editor, you are given quite a bit of freedom. It operates much like a word processor and gives you the privilege of typing what you want, where you want it. But, just in case you feel a little lost, try using some of these suggestions I've listed below:

① Start with typing a title *(i.e. FAX)*, use the button with the letters (**ab|**) on it to type your title.

② Use the menu bar, especially the **Insert** option. I think you will find it sets the entire cover page up for you.

③ You can use the mouse to resize and relocate any objects on the cover page you want.

④ You can also include pictures within a cover page. To do this, look in the **Insert** selection on the menu bar and click on the word **Object...**, doing so will open up a new window. From there, you will want to select the **ClipArt Gallery** and then choose a picture.

Figure 15.3
Inserting a picture

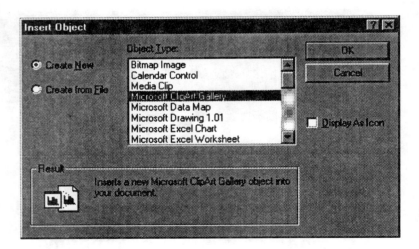

⑤ Don't forget to save your cover page, so you will be able to use it in the future.

After a little experimenting, you should be a master. If you work for a large company, you can use the cover page editor to design a cover page which proudly displays your company logo. You can also create distinct cover pages for each faxes. In the end, I think you will realize what a valuable tool this is, and use it when ever you need to fax someone.

Creating & Sending Faxes

We are now ready to create and send a fax. However, when creating a fax, there are a few questions you must be aware of.

First, who are you going to send it to? And is that person ready to receive it? Chances are, if you happen to be sending it to a large company, they own a separate fax machine with a dedicated line, so timing won't be an issue. But, on the other hand, if you are sending a fax to a friend who only owns one computer with one phone line, you will want to make sure they will be ready to receive your fax when the time comes.

When faxing someone, the first thing you want to do is open the **Accessories** folder and click on the directory named **Fax** (just like you did with the cover page editor). From there, simply pick **Compose New Fax**, and you are ready to begin.

Doing this for the first time may seem a little slow, but even from the start you should notice how simple it is. Microsoft really went out of its way to make sure they didn't complicate anything. Once you start to compose a new fax, a little picture of a fax machine will appear on the Taskbar. This means the modem inside your computer has been activated, however, your phone line has not. So if you only happen to have one phone line, you can still use it at this point. Unfortunately, when you are transmitting a fax with only one phone line, the modem will tie it up. This makes it difficult to communicate with the receiving party. I suggest in these cases, to use smoke signals, congo drums or strobe lights.

After an introduction screen, you will find yourself at the first important window. This window's main responsibility is to get the fax number and name of the person of whom you are trying to fax. The only really important section in this window is the **Fax #** and the **Name**, everything else is optional. Although, if you do leave out some of this optional information, you may notice it missing in the cover page; but the fax will make it to its destination.

Figure 15.4
Choosing a Cover Letter for the Fax

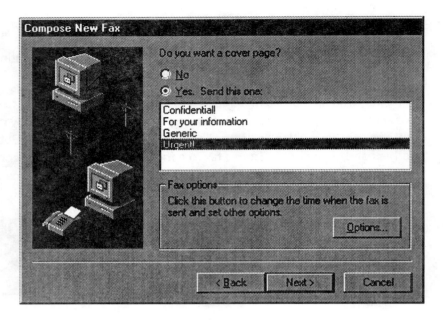

The next window, shown above, sets up the cover page for the fax. From here you can select one of the Windows' cover pages or one of your own. If you are sending a fax to a friend and want to save some trees, you can choose to have no cover page at all.

In addition, Windows furnishes you with four different cover letter styles to choose from. The table below gives a brief description of each.

Cover page	What it means
Confidential!	Microsoft's way of sending secret information
For your Information	An informational fax
General purposes	A simple cover page for all occasions
Urgent!	A 9-1-1 fax

Keep in mind, these are only cover pages and have absolutely no effect on how the fax is sent. So, selecting an **Urgent!** cover letter style, will not send a fax any faster than if you had chosen **FYI**.

Figure 15.5
Making the actual fax

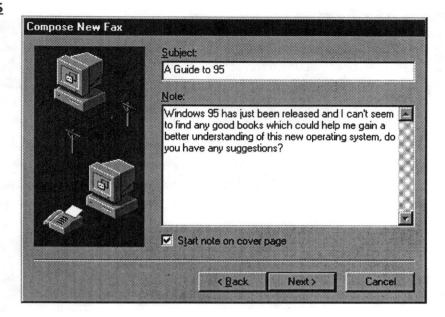

The window shown above, is the window you have been waiting for. It is in this window where you are allowed to type the message you want to fax. It is considered common courtesy to include the subject matter in the top section of the window, but it can be excluded if you prefer. In fact, this entire step can be left out, if so desired. But why? One good reason for leaving this window empty is when faxing a picture, or a file (a document). Those kind of options are allowed in the next window (after pressing the **Next>** button).

After completing all the material information, the only thing left to do is to send it. This is done when you click on the word **Finish>**. When sending a fax, you will be unable to use the phone, assuming you only have one phone line. Luckily, these faxes are fast and take little or no time to transmit. You should actually hear the phone ringing and connecting. Then you can watch the status of the transmission on the computer until it is completed.

Figure 15.6
Sending a fax

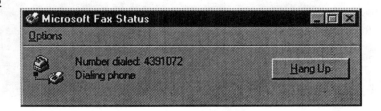

Receiving Faxes

Receiving a fax with Windows 95 is not as automatic as it should be. Because Windows needs an uninterrupted phone line in order to detect incoming faxes, the fax program is not very practical in most households. Fortunately, faxes are not very common. So, there is little point in having a devoted phone line on all day just to receive one. The best thing to do, is have your computer ready when you know a fax is coming and here is how to do it.

Start with opening up the **Accessories** folder and clicking on the **Fax** directory. From there you can start the **Request a Fax** program. This program will activate your modem.

In addition, what this program does is allow you to dial into a fax information service and receive faxes. To do this you must know the phone number of the fax information service in your local area. I suggest looking in a phone book to find the one nearest you. Upon obtaining the correct number, you can go about receiving a fax much in the same way you would send one.

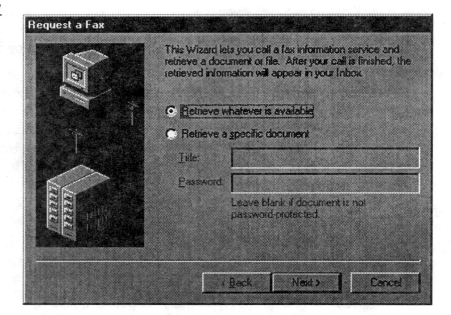

Figure 15.7
Setting up to receive a Fax from an information service

Microsoft has always done things ahead of its time and this is just another example of that. These so-called fax information services will no doubt be much more popular and common in the future.

There are other ways of receiving faxes which work a lot more directly. If you know when a fax is coming, you can receive it by double-clicking on the little picture of a fax machine in the Taskbar. This picture is always present when any of the programs in the **fax** directory are running.

After clicking on the picture of the fax machine in the Taskbar, the **Fax Status** dialog box will appear. This box lets the fax machine answer the phone when the **Answer Now** button is pushed in.

Figure 15.8
Receiving a Fax, using a more direct method

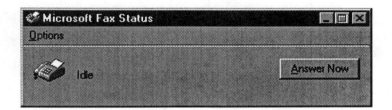

Once the phone starts ringing, simply click on the **Answer Now** button and the fax machine will receive the message. After the fax has been transmitted, it will be save in the **Inbox** icon.

Inbox

Sending and receiving faxes are not the only thing a modem is good for. Another more popular use of today's modems is networking and cruising the Super Informational Highway. You'll see how similar they are to faxing, only taking it one step further. I will discuss these topics in the next chapter, entitled the **Microsoft Network**.

The Microsoft Network

CHAPTER 16

The Microsoft Network is the newest on-line service available to Windows 95 users. Other companies like America On-line, CompuServe and Prodigy have been providing this service for years. Now, it is Microsoft's turn to enter the market and it does so with a bit of an advantage. You see, every copy of Windows 95 is also going to automatically include access to the Microsoft Network. As a Windows user, all you have to decide is whether or not to use it. In either case, this chapter is about the Microsoft Network and is designed to help you understand it better.

On-line Networks

What is an on-line network? A network is a collection of computers tied together to create a single powerful system. This structure is then capable of performing tasks which each individual system could not achieve. An on-line network is very similar, only on a larger and more commercial scale.

Networks mostly include closely nit computers. You may find them in a business office or as large systems bound together by phone lines spanning the length of our nation. The term network is very broad and can really depict many different images. The kind of networks this chapter is going to discuss are called on-line Networks.

On-line Networks first began to appear in the late eighties. They packaged themselves as futuristic catalogs, giving their users the ability to purchase everything from a car to household groceries. Most of these early offers seemed a little too extravagant and didn't especially appeal to most computer users.

For starters, a modem was needed to gain access. Even though modems are quite common today, a few years ago, they weren't as popular. Initially, modems were very slow and difficult to install. They weren't designed to handle the large amounts of data an on-line service could generate.

However, after years of development and research, modems have finally reached their golden years. Today's modems can work 100 times faster than their predecessors and can be easily installed into computers within minutes. With advancements like these, the popularity of modems grew and so did on-line services. Another reason for the renewed interest in on-line services has been the Internet.

The Internet is the latest craze to hit the computer industry. It seems everyone is trying to get connected. From homepages to hyperlinks, the internet is much more than just an on-line network.

http://www.wolfenet.com/~jwhelan/

The Internet

The Information Super Highway of the 90's isn't referring to a road of pavement stretching across the nation. Instead, it is a road of phone lines connecting the world and it is called the **Internet**. The Internet has been around for years, but only lately has it become extremely popular. One reason for its popularity is the easy ability to access it. This is very apparent in Windows 95 where the click of one icon can get you directly on this super highway.

The Internet was originally established by the government during the second world war. It was started by an agency called **ARPA**, which stands for the Advanced Research Project Agency. Initially known as **DARPA** (the word *defense* was later removed), this agency was responsible for revealing many advancements in computers which are quite common today. The mouse was invented by this agency, as well as the first C.A.D. (Computer Aided Design) programs.

Back when the Internet was developed, it was rather boring and contained no flashy graphics at all. However, throughout the years, the Internet has grown. Fueled by users around the world, today's Internet is one of the most valuable commodities on this planet. Yet, it is owned by no one and using it doesn't cost any money. The catch is, you have to be able to access it.

Accessing the Internet, or getting connected, is not as easy as you might think. Because of its age, the Internet was written in an older programming language called **UNIX**. Few, if any computers in homes today have the capacity to understand this complex language. In simple terms, most household computers are not compatible with the Internet. Another problem is getting physically connected with the Internet, because it isn't owned by any one person.

The way to work around these problems is to subscribe to an access provider and use an Internet browser. An access provider can allow any personal computers access to the Internet. These providers come in many different shapes and sizes. They include large companies, like America On-line and smaller independent ones.

Independent access providers are a good way for people to use the Internet. These independent companies often charge small fees and usually provide good services. The library too is a good place to look for the Internet. Since the early nineties, many libraries have updated their inventory to include computers with access to the Internet. Microsoft itself also allows its users access to the Internet, by using their network accompanied with another program they manufactuer.

What Microsoft has to offer

Try not to confuse on-line networks with the Internet: they are two completely different services. On-line networks, like America On-line, CompuServe, Prodigy and Microsoft Network are usually smaller, more tamer versions of the Internet. Whereas with the Internet itself, there are no rules.

Microsoft offers both services to its users. But, they are in different packages. Access to the Internet comes in a supplementary program called **Microsoft Plus**. This program uses a browser called the **Internet Explorer** and a preestablish connection through the Microsoft Network. Whereas, with the individual Microsoft Network which comes with Windows 95, only allows limited access. I will spend the remainder of this chapter discussing it. For more information about the Internet Explorer or Microsoft Plus, check out **Chapter 20**.

The Microsoft Network, or **MSN**, is not automatically installed on a computer with first installation of Windows 95. During the installation, you are asked if you want to join the Microsoft Network. At this time it is not necessary to respond yes, since you can always install MSN any time, after the initial installation.

Once installed, MSN will then ask you to sign up. It is at this point where a credit card number is needed. During this process, you need to provide a billing address, a phone number and some other additional information. The procedure takes about 2 minutes, depending slightly on the speed of your modem.

Most on-line Networks, like MSN and America Online require a credit card number for membership. One advantage of an independent access provider is they may be willing to take a check or money order.

After its installation, Windows 95 sets up an icon for MSN. This allows you access to the network with only one click. MSN comes with lots of substance and is accessible in more than 35 countries. Here is a list of some of the benefits and attractions you will find on MSN:

- ☑ Electronic mail, or email
- ☑ Bulletin boards
- ☑ "Chat rooms"
- ☑ File libraries
- ☑ Internet newsgroups
- ☑ Down-loadable files
- ☑ Technical support, and a whole lot more

The Microsoft Network

Most of the features mentioned above are offered in other on-line networks, as well. What makes MSN unique is the way its package fits together. By grouping related material together, MSN is able to cover a broad range of subjects. This includes everything from sports and entertainment to education and business. The range is so large, that it is difficult to describe and is better experiencing.

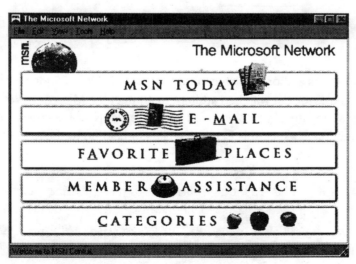

Figure 16.1
MSN Central, otherwise known as the Welcome Screen

MSN offers much more than any single computer could ever handle. You can literally spend hours going from window to window. It has information on endless topics and is real easy to get lost in. So, on the next few pages, let me give you some useful hints to help you navigate around this network.

Hint #1   Remember your password

Each user is given a user name and a password. Obviously, it is very important not to lose either your user name or password, because obtaining another one can be quite difficult. On the other hand, it is equally as important not to advertise your password either, because if someone obtained it, they could sign on as you. The reason behind this is, your user name and password represent your account, not your computer.

Figure 16.2
The Sign In window for MSN

Signing In is a chore which cannot be avoided. After Windows receives a user name and password, it will then attempt to contact the Microsoft Network via the computer's modem. If you own one phone line, MSN will occupy it during its on-line connection; so keep this in mind, while connecting to the network.

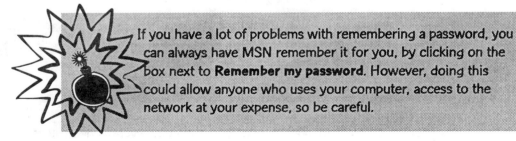

If you have a lot of problems with remembering a password, you can always have MSN remember it for you, by clicking on the box next to **Remember my password**. However, doing this could allow anyone who uses your computer, access to the network at your expense, so be careful.

Hint #2   Be careful what you click on

Any icon with a folder on it is safe to click on. Folders represent entrances to other topics. If an icon does not have a folder in it, then you have reached a file or a program. If it is a file, clicking on it will cause your computer to download the file. Downloading files take a fair amount of time and hard disk space.

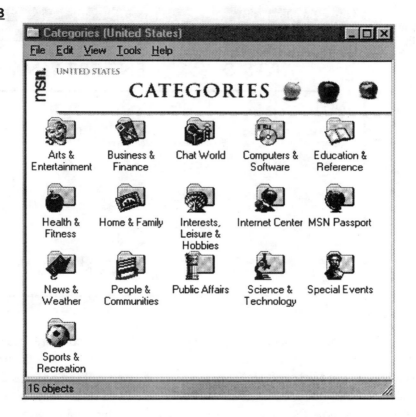

Figure 16.3
The Categories window in MSN

Notice all the icons in the window above have folders. This means they all provide access to other windows. In the window above, each icon represents a different topic and clicking on it will take you to a different place.

As you venture further into MSN, the topics tend to narrow down. This way, you eventually end up in a window where all the icons relate to the same topic, like music or football. These windows are also called **rooms** and each icon represents a **door**.

The window below was produced after clicking on the **Arts & Entertainment** icon from the preceding window on the previous page. Notice in this window some of the icons do not contain folders in them. These icons represent programs and clicking on them will activate the program, just like the ones on the Windows desktop.

Figure 16.4
The Arts & Entertainment window in MSN

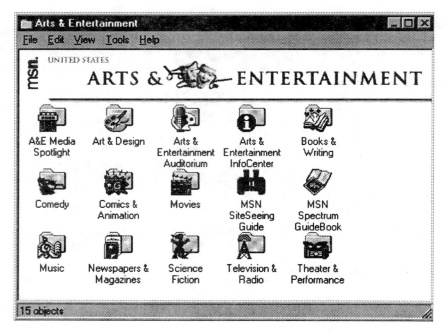

Some icons will appear with no pictures at all. These icons are files and clicking on them will cause your computer to start automatically downloading them. Downloading on the Microsoft Network is essentially free, but the process does take valuable time and hard disk space. In some cases, you might may be unaware of exactly how large the file is, you are downloading. This could result in system problems. So, as a rule of thumb, always use caution when clicking on icons.

Figure 16.5
A downloadable file

Sam Kinison

Hint #3   Do not get lost in the Network

It only takes a couple of clicks to get lost on MSN. Sometimes even the computer will not be able to keep up with you and it too could get lost. So, before things get too confusing, slow down and remember where you came from.

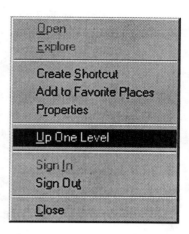

The easiest way to do this is by using the menu bar that comes with MSN. At the top of every window in the network is a menu bar and you can use it to help guide yourself through the network. If you find yourself too deep in a topic, use the **Up One Level** command in the **File** pull down menu. This command takes you back one step and if you continue using it, you will get back to where you originally started.

In addition, if your journey through the Microsoft Network brings to a great location, which you would like to save. With MSN, you can by creating a shortcut. This way you won't have to search for it again on the network.

To create a Shortcut, start with highlighting the location you want to save. Then click on the **Create Shortcut** command in the **File** pull down menu. This will automatically produce a shortcut icon on the Windows desktop.

Figure 16.6
Creating a Shortcut in MSN

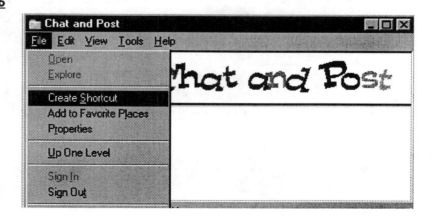

e-mail

Electronic mail is another great advantage of on-line services. It gives you access to the world at a very small price. Electronic mail, more commonly known as e-mail, is available on the Microsoft Network and is housed in a separate program called **Microsoft Exchange**. This e-mail program has two great features:

① It gives you the ability to e-mail anyone who has an e-mail address, regardless of which network they belong to. This means you can talk to your friends on America On-line or Prodigy, as long as they have an e-mail address. It does not matter who issued it to them.

② In addition, Microsoft Exchange can be used even when you are not connected to the network. This means you can write long messages without having to worry about any expenses. The only time you need the network is when the e-mail is actually sent. Until then, the message just waits in the mail box until the next time you connect to the network and then it's sent automatically.

Microsoft Exchange works with the Microsoft Network to provide you with a complete electronic post office. It is easy to use and operates a lot like a word processor. Let's take a closer look

Inbox

Figure 16.7
Microsoft Exchange

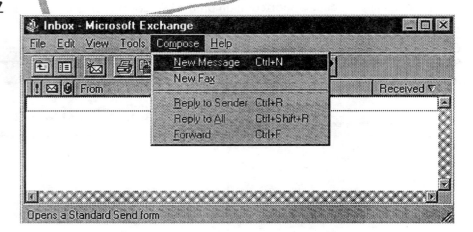

Start by clicking on the Inbox icon. Once the program has opened, you will find creating a message to be quite simple. Unfortunately, like in real life, before you can send someone a letter you must know their address. E-mail addresses are a little strange at first, but much like their real life counter-parts, they do have a consistent format.

An E-mail address should start with a **User Name**, followed by an @ symbol, then the **Network Id** and completed with an **Extension**. Keep in mind, e-mail addresses are case-sensitive!

Here is an example: **johnwhel@wolfenet.com**

Microsoft Exchange allows you to create e-mail, read it and reply to letters users sent you. It even lets you store special messages in folders which you can name yourself, as shown in the diagram below.

Figure 16.8
Storing e-mail with Microsoft Exchange

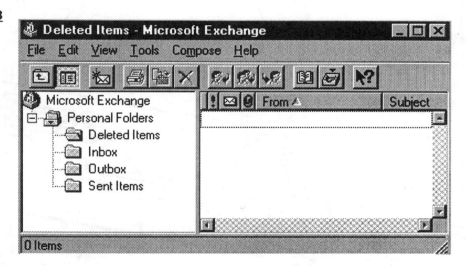

Using e-mail takes a little practice at first, but someday it may replace the real thing. However, until then, I am going to continue to collect Elvis stamps.

Microsoft Exchange even works with internal networks, like the ones you might find at an office. It is a great program with lots of neat features. It includes a spell-checker, address books and much more. After using it once or twice, I think you might find e-mail as cool as sending notes in grade school. It is really the same thing, but in a much bigger school.

Microsoft Exchange is only a small part of the package, the rest of the Microsoft Network is better off experiencing on your own, it's full potential could never fit in just one book, let alone a single chapter.

Keep in mind, currently Microsoft charges by the hour for its network time. Other network companies set flat fees and allow unlimited access. However, Microsoft is not one of them. So, try to limit your time on the network to only quality pursuits. Don't waste your time downloading worthless files or jumping around from window to window.

Plug n Play

CHAPTER 17

One of the most advertised features of Windows 95, is **Plug and Play**. The original idea behind Plug and Play was to allow users to "plug" in new hardware devices and then proceed to use them, without having to mess with any of the hassles surrounding the configuration. With Windows 95, users can exercise at least half of this routine, by using Plug and Play to handle the configuration. Unfortunately, the actual installation must still be done manually, since most of today's systems are not set up to have components plugged into them.

However, with the advent of Windows 95, many computer builders are designing systems which have Plug and Play-like features built-in, in order to achieve Microsoft's original vision. Someday every system will be physically suited to handle Plug and Play. But, until then, you will still have to install the new devices yourself and let Windows 95 do the rest.

Plug and Play in the Past

In the past, installing new components into a computer was considered a major undertaking. You were expected to play the role of a technician, without any of the experience. Most installations involved a two step process with each step presenting its own problems.

First, you had to worry about the physical installation, knowing where and how to install the component. As if that wasn't bad enough, you then had to deal with the system configuration, which could be as difficult or worse to figure out than the actual installation.

All the complications of installation usually lead users to one of the three paths outlined below:

① Have a trained technician install the component for you. This is a very safe option, but also an expensive one. Most technicians charge around $48 an hour and often throw in extra fees.

② Install the component yourself. This option is not always as easy as many retail packages and brochures make it out to be. Installing any component on a computer takes a lot of patience and a fair amount of intelligence. If you don't know what you are doing outside the computer, chances are you will do much worse inside one. On the other hand, this option doesn't cost any extra cash and can be a real good learning experience, if you don't mind sacrificing your system in the name of education.

③ Buy a computer with the component pre-installed. This is the ideal option, unfortunately, it isn't always very practical. Chances are, with today's technology, even the most advance system is going to need upgrading within a couple of years. My computer itself, became outdated within months, and I had to resort to one of the other options mentioned above.

Computer components, like modems, CD-ROMS, hard drives and sound cards, are designed to be replaced or upgraded. They are not necessarily permanent structures and are housed in interchangeable locations within the computer.

Some of these components occupy slots on a system's motherboard. The number of slots can vary with each system and usually correspond to the numbers of external grooves on the back of a computer. These slots are called **expansion slots** and are designed to hold all kinds of devices. In fact, with the exception of the keyboard, any other external device must run through one of these slots in order to reach the inside of a computer.

In the future, the intention is to dispose of these slots and have all the external devices plug straight into a computer, much like a pair of head phones would plug into a Walkman. Then Plug and Play would take on a role which suits its name.

Plug and Play

With Plug and Play, Microsoft has gotten one step closer to making computers appear less complicated. By lessening the technicalities associated with its operating system, computers can begin to function more like other household appliances. Then, they will be accessible to more people and not demand such a high level of intelligence. This is a long process and will take many years to complete, since from the beginning, computers have always preferred to be confusing. But, one important element of this goal is Plug and Play. Here is how it works.

It starts with a new device (*which can include almost anything*). The first step is to install it. Windows 95 assumes you can do that much. It is a pretty high assumption, but it is one you will have to live with, at least until Plug and Play-like devices are manufactured.

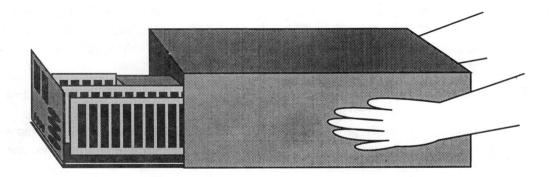

After the installation, a connection must be made so Windows can recognize the device. This connection is usually made automatically when Windows performs a system check, but in any case, it doesn't hurt to follow the procedures.

The closest thing you will find to **Plug and Play** is in the Control Panel. Plug and Play is not a program, is a concept. The concept itself, is captured in a program called **Add New Hardware** and you will find its icon located within the Control Panel. Therefore, to install new hardware, you will want to double-click on that icon.

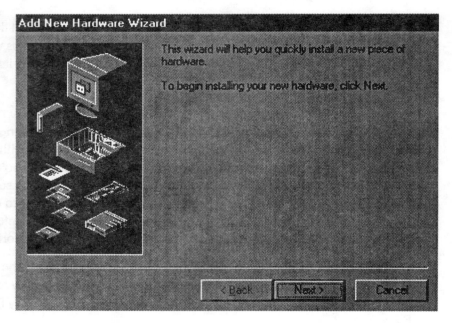

Figure 17.1
The Add New Hardware Wizard

Double-clicking on the Add New Hardware icon will start the Add New Hardware Wizard. A **wizard** is Microsoft's way of helping users out with complicated tasks. With this wizard, we get a hand on installing new hardware. The first window which appears is just an introduction window and can be quickly skipped by clicking on the **Next>** button.

The next thing the wizard will do, is ask if you want it to perform a system test. It uses this test to find any newly installed hardware components. Once it finds one, it will then determine the correct settings and device drivers for that component. This step, was previously missing from earlier versions of Windows and was left as the user's responsibility.

Figure 17.2
The wizard will attempt to locate new hardware

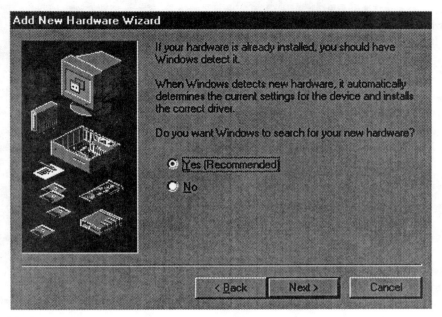

Before the wizard begins its search through the computer for newly installed components, it is a good idea to close all other programs. Because the search itself is very resource intensive.

During this time, a computer may experience lock ups and appear to be non-responsive. There will also be a lot of disk activity. This is a natural occurrence and should not be considered as a problem, although if it lasts longer than two or three minutes, a system re-boot may be in order. During the search, an indicator is provided to give you an idea of how long the search will take.

In the case where the search comes up empty or the component isn't considered to be newly installed, you will be asked to help Windows out. This is done by manually choosing the device from a list of components to install. Windows provides the list and it is the same regardless of what your computer may or not have. All you need to do is find the component on the list and highlight it. Then click on the **Next>** button, as shown on the next page.

Figure 17.3
Telling the Wizard what to Install

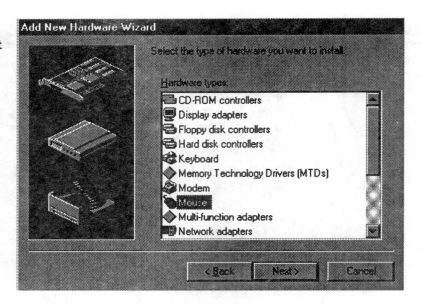

Once a device is selected, Windows may ask for some more assistance. It could inquire about device drivers, since it was unable to locate the components in the first place. From here it may begin a downward spiral towards a botched configuration accompanied with a failed installation.

Figure 17.4
The Wizard is inquiring about device drivers

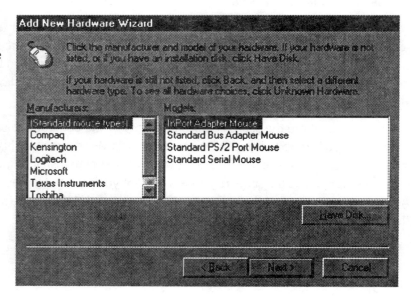

The whole idea behind Plug and Play was to avoid dealing with configuration. If the Add New Hardware wizard starts inquiring about device drivers and other technical attributes, chances are you either don't have the component installed correctly or it isn't supported by Windows 95.

What's next?

There is a good possibility you will never use the Add New Hardware program, commercially known as Plug and Play. Since Windows 95 does a system check, every time it is started and then makes the appropriate adjustments. This feature really only applies to future applications of Windows, when the concept of Plug and Play is a closer fit to its name.

Plug and Play is a feature which will probably gain more respect and use as the industry grows. The main idea behind Plug and Play was to develop an industry standard. As you may be aware of, the computer industry sadly lacks standards. With Windows 95, standards are becoming a more important part of the system, than they have been in the past. This is one evolution which may go beyond Windows.

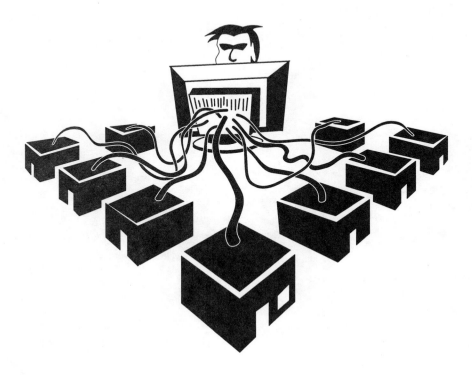

The Windows 95 Wrap-up

Tricks, Hints and Traps

CHAPTER 18

This chapter is intended to reveal every Windows secret known to mankind, or at least known to this author. Like many software programs, Windows 95 was created with a few hidden inconsistencies and discrepancies. I am not talking about world-altering events here, just little things which can be fun to explore. As you may have guessed, this chapter is divided into three sections, appropriately named; Windows **tricks**, helpful **hints** and deadly **traps**. All three sections are designed to give you a head start with Windows 95 and help explore some of its mysteries.

Windows Tricks

Every program has its secrets. Some are small and go unnoticed, while others are abused and destroy any challenging aspect of a program. In either case, it is only a matter of time before the secret gets out. Microsoft has spent countless hours and money to make sure its latest version of Windows is secret-free, but did they succeed?

What is a secret? A secret is something kept in concealment and from the knowledge of others. This is an open-minded definition of the word secret and can include, depending upon the user's lack of knowledge, almost any aspect in Windows.

However, true Windows secrets are few and far between. Within the next couple of pages, I hope to uncover as many of them as possible. After which, I describe some helpful hints. Let's begin with some easy ones and go from there.

Secret#1 (seeing additional information)

To see additional information about any object in Windows, simply put the mouse pointer on top of it. For example, many buttons in Windows can be described first, by putting the mouse pointer on top of them. The description ranges with each object. This principle also holds true in many other programs as well. In most cases, Windows likes to tell its users what to do next. This is designed to help beginners develop more confidence in their decisions.

Figure 18.1
Windows telling us what its icons do

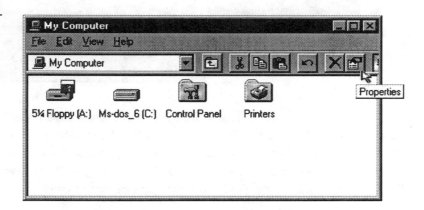

Another way to view more information about a certain icon is to click on it, using the **right-hand** mouse button. This automatically opens a list of options, which can be performed on that icon. The list often includes options like Open, Explore, Delete or Properties. Performing any one of these functions can be considered a short cut.

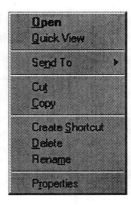

This works with any object in Windows 95. Try clicking the right-hand mouse button on the Taskbar or the system clock. Either way, you will open up new possibilities or new short cuts.

Secret#2 (helping Windows get Started)

There is a small place in Windows which escapes many users' eyes. It is a little known directory called **StartUp** and can be a real neat place to store programs. Any program stored in this location will automatically start when Windows itself is started. For instance, if you put the game of Solitaire in this directory, it will be waiting for you every time you turn on the computer.

Figure 18.2
The StartUp Directory

Putting the right programs in this directory can be a real advantage. You should put programs which are used a lot there. In addition, some programs are designed to always be running, like the **Resource meter**. If you put a program like this in the StartUp directory, you won't have to worry about starting it. If you own Microsoft Office, it is automatically installed in the StartUp directory as well.

However, If you want to add programs to the StartUp directory, you must do it through the **Taskbar**. To add one, follow these simple steps.

❶ Click on **Settings** in the start menu and then on **Taskbar...**

❷ When the Taskbar Properties window opens, click on the division entitled **Start Menu Programs**.

❸ Then click on the **Advanced...** button.

❹ The next step is to select the program you want to put in the StartUp directory. Then drag it, with the mouse, to the StartUp directory and drop it in. You can repeat this step for all the programs you wish to add. When you are finished, close the window and click on the **OK** button.

Tricks, Hints and Traps 237

Figure 18.3
Adding a program to the StartUp Directory

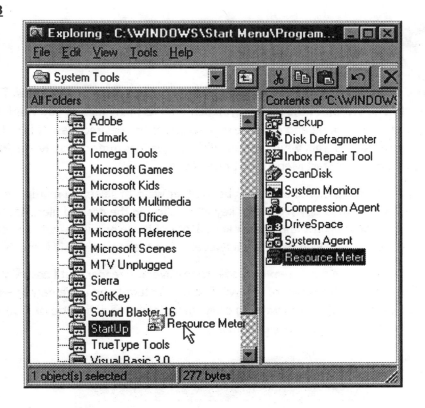

❺ After completing these steps, the next time you start Windows 95, you should see the additional programs which were added to this directory, start as well.

If the **StartUp** directory becomes too full, it may make turning on a computer into a momentous event. In general, Windows 95 has enough things to do, when it is started. Consequently, filling up this directory only makes things worse. So, try not to over use it!

Secret#3 (Grabbing Multiple Files)

A unique addition to Windows 95 is its ability to grab multiple files. This means with one swoop of the mouse, you can grab as many files as you want. All you have to do is point and drag the mouse across the desired files. This only holds true in any program which can handle multiple files, unfortunately, the **Programs** section of the Start Menu is not one of them.

In the past, there has always been other ways of selecting multiple files. One way was to hold down the **Ctrl** key while clicking the desired files. Another way was to use the **shift** and **cursor** keys. Both of these primitive methods can still be used today with Windows 95, however using the mouse solely is much easier.

This feature may seem unusable to the average reader, but I assure you, there are situations where you will find this feature to be extremely practical. For example, when you want to copy multiple files to a diskette or if you want to select multiple fonts for a document.

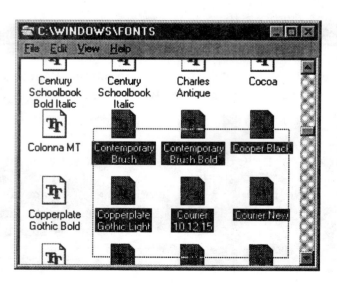

Figure 18.4
Selecting Multiple Files

The files can only be selected in a rectangular formation, so make sure all the files are close together. If by chance, you need to pick an extra file which has strayed from the pack, you can hold down the **Ctrl** key and select it too.

Tricks, Hints and Traps

Secret#4 (Working with the Disk Drives)

All kinds of drives need to routinely undergo an occasional maintenance check. Since they are mechanical pieces, which are used more often than any other device on a computer, they are more prone to damage.

Much like an engine needs tuning or an occasional oil change, the disk drives on a computer also need frequent attention, because of their size and delicate nature. In particular, the internal drives (i.e. the hard drives) need special attention because they house such important information. Any impairment which damages a hard drive, also would destroy all the files on that drive. This would be like a simple flat tire, causing an entire automobile to crash and get demolished.

One way to avoid potential problems is to use some of the built in short cuts for managing disk drives. These short-cuts are found in **My Computer**. To activate them, open My Computer and click the right-hand mouse button, on the drive you wish to examine. Then select the **Properties** option from the pull-down menu, as shown below.

Figure 18.5
Selecting a a drive to check, with the Properties option

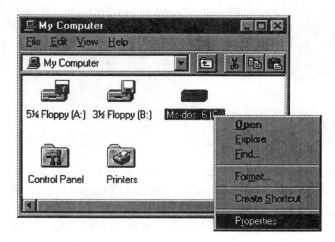

In the diagram on the previous page, I selected the **C:** drive, but I could have easily chosen a floppy drive instead. The only catch is the drive has to be able to store information, so a CD-ROM drive would not work, since it cannot store data. Once a drive is chosen, select the **Properties** option and the system tools will be at your disposal.

Figure 18.6
The System Tools in the Properties window

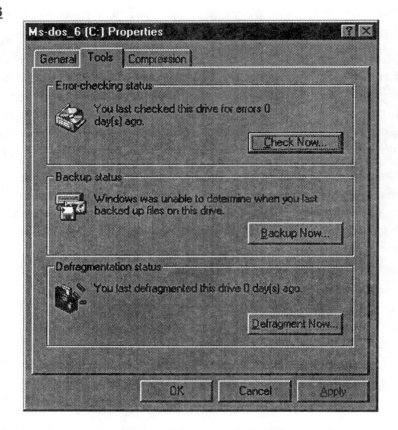

In the window shown above, you can select from a variety of System Tools. These tools include an **error-checker**, a **backup utility** and a **defragmenter**. If you think you may have seen these tools before, then you are right. After all, these are the same programs you would find in the **System Tools** folder in the **Accessories** directory. The only difference is the way we got to them. That is why they call it a short-cut!

Tricks, Hints and Traps

Here is a brief description of each of these tools. You can also find more information about these tools in **Chapter 12**, which is the chapter about Utilities.

- ☑ The **Error-Checker**. This tool scans the disk for any errors and then can correct them. These errors are usual caused by inconsistent file sizes and stray data. If they are ignored for long enough, these errors could cause a major system crash. But until then, they will only slow a system down. Subsequently, the Error-Checker is not considered to be a virus-scanner.

- ☑ The **Backup Tool**. This tool copies the contents of the selected drive onto a storable media. In most case, the backups would be kept on diskettes or a data tape. With this utility, you are allowed to choose what files get copied and where to put them. The program also notes the date and time, so you can track when the last backup was made.

- ☑ The **Defragmenter**. Not to be confused with the Error-checker, the Defragmenter performs a scan on a disk to make sure the data on it is stored in the most efficient places. When it finds data which has been separated, it takes the data and puts it in the correct adjacent locations. The entire process takes about five minutes and results in a smoother and faster running operating system.

CHAPTER EIGHTEEN

Secret #5 Using Secret Passwords

For the users who think big-brother is watching them all the time, Windows 95 comes with the ability to operate with passwords. This means, only people who know a certain password can use your computer and if they don't know it, then the computer will essentially lock up.

Besides the James Bond features of this application, it can also be used to support **multiple users**. By giving different passwords to each user, you can make one computer operate like a small network. Similar to the computer you may have seen at work, where workers log on to the system at different terminals. Regardless of what terminal they are at, as long as they use the correct password, they always appear to be in the same environment. By using passwords in Windows 95, you can achieve the same effect.

To give your system a password, follow these simple steps:

❶ Click on the **Passwords** icon in the **Control Panel**. It is the icon with the keys on it. This will open the Password Properties window.

❷ The **Password Properties window** is where everything dealing with passwords is controlled. It is like the Central Intelligence Headquarters for Windows. In the window shown on the next page, you can customize the settings of the different users. It is divided into four options, which can be a little confusing at first.

TRICKS, HINTS AND TRAPS 243

Figure 18.7
The Password Properties window

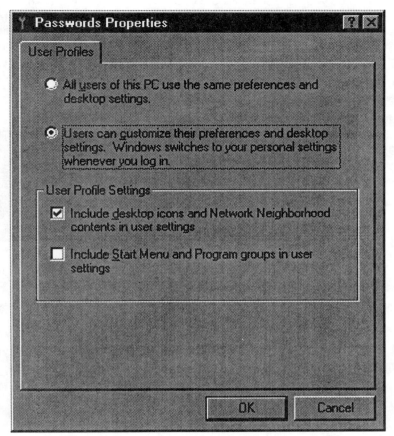

☑ The first option says all users will see the same layout. This is the box, you would want to check if you do <u>not</u> want to use passwords. It is also the same way you would cancel passwords.

☑ The next option allows users to have a password. This allows any user to individually customize their Windows sessions without effecting any one else on the system. This is how one computer can support multiple users.

☑ The last two options are only available if the second option is chosen. These options describe what elements in the Windows layout will be different among users or sessions. The first of these options deals with the shortcuts on the desktop, like My Computer and the Recycler; and the second one deals with the programs in the Taskbar. If you want each user to use his own desktop, I suggest having both options marked!

❸ Once you have selected the option to use, click on the **OK** button. In order for the passwords to take effect, you must restart the computer.

❹ After restarting the computer, you will be asked to sign on. Since this is your first time signing on with passwords, you will also be asked to **confirm** your password, by typing it again. This assures you a typo won't leave you locked out of your system.

Figure 18.8
Signing on to Windows 95, with a password

All users, must select a username and a password. It is important to remember them, since you will need them every time you use Windows! If you want to add a new user to the system, simply select a new username and a new password.

Subsequentially, using passwords doesn't affect any programs in Windows at all. In fact, you will hardly even notice any differences, except when you start Windows and when you finished it. In the **Shut Down...** procedures, you will be given an extra option; to log on as a different user. This only restarts Windows, so a new user can log on.

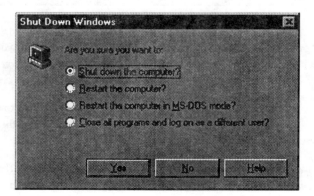

Figure 18.9
Windows Shutting Down with Passwords

Secret#6 (Sending Files quickly)

Windows 95 can work more as a tool than an operating system. It has the ability to handle many tasks which are completely independent of its system duties. For instance, moving files around a system can be confusing and difficult. Mainly because, it isn't always clear which file is being moved and where it is going. Wouldn't it be nice if you could grab a file and move it anywhere quickly?

There is a small program in Windows which does just that, unfortunately it is very hard to find it. It is called **SendTo** and it does not have an icon. So, in order to start it, you must use the **Run...** Command in the Start Menu.

Figure 18.10
The Run dialog box

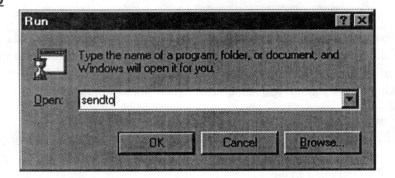

Once you click on the **Run...** command, Windows will ask you for a program to open. Simply type the command **"sendto"** and Windows will go find the correct program as well as start it.

SendTo is a unique program, at first glance, it appears to be a rather plain window. But what makes this window different, is that it allows you to send files.

Figure 18.11
Sending Files

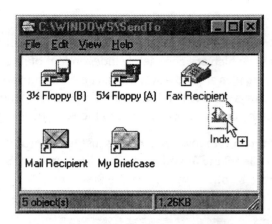

To use it, start by putting a file in the window and dropping it on the icon where you want the data to go. To make things even easier, leave this window open at the top of the screen. Then use it, as you open up documents or other programs. By clicking and dragging, you can quickly send data to almost any location. Below, is a list of some typical examples.

- ☑ If you want to send a company a copy of your resume, simply grab the file (document) and drop it on the Fax Recipient.
- ☑ If you want to e-mail your friend a copy of a picture, just grab the file (picture) and drop it on the Mail Recipient.
- ☑ If you want to copy some documents on a diskette, simply grab the document and drop it on one of the drives.

When a file is dropped on an icon in the **SendTo** window, it will automatically start the program associated with that icon. This mainly pertains to the fax and mail recipients since phone numbers and e-mail addresses are needed.

Helpful hints

Using Windows 95 is not as easy as it may appear. To a new user, many of its popular features and so-called simple arrangements may seem puzzling at best.

Personally, I have been using Windows myself for years and along the way I have picked up some helpful hints. Listed below are some suggestions or hints about how to make Windows 95 run a lot smoother. The list I have prepared, covering the next few pages, contains a few suggestions which may help struggling Windows users.

Hint #1:

Avoid double-clicking on icons, simply select the icon with the mouse and hit the **Enter** key. Double-clicking takes too long and can be easily misinterpreted by Windows. In the diagram below, accessing the 5$^{1/4}$ Floppy drive is as easy as hitting the **Enter** key. Because after an icon has been highlighted, it is ready to be executed.

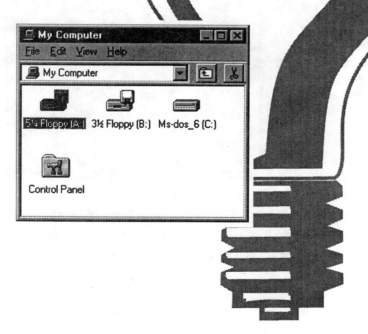

Figure 18.12
Selecting a drive from My Computer

Hint #2:

Contrary to popular belief, experienced Windows users handle the mouse as seldom as possible. The **Alt** and **cursor** keys make good substitutes. They provide much more timely and precise actions. Also, when running multiple programs, try using **Alt +Tab** instead of the mouse, to switch among them. Here are some other keyboard shortcuts:

Key(s)	Description
Alt+Esc	Switches to next task
Ctrl+Esc	Opens the Start Menu
F1	Select any part of Windows, press F1 and receive help.
F2	Select any icon in Windows, press F2 and you can change its name
F3	Opens the Find window, which helps locate programs and files
Alt+F4	Closes an open window. If no windows are open, then it closes Windows 95
Ctrl+C	Copies a selection to the Clipboard. An easy way to remember this, is to think of C as in Copy
Ctrl+X	Cuts a selection to the Clipboard. An easy way to remember this, is to think of Xing or crossing something out
Ctrl+V	Pastes a selection from the Clipboard. An easy way to remember this, is to think of adding a word to a sentence like: Windows is ˅ neat. Really

In addition, you may want to review the last part of Chapter 9. There you will find special key strokes, designed to simulate the movements of the mouse.

Hint #3:

Remember to utilize the menu bars. Since all Windows programs have similar features, such as **File**, **Edit**, **View**, **Help** or whatever the case; learning to master these controls will prove not only helpful in Windows, but in other programs as well.

Hint #4:

Try leaving your computer on, day and night. A computer does not require a lot of energy and can perform useful self-diagnostic tests on its files while unused. Remember too, businesses operate 24 hours a day with computers going non stop.

Please keep in mind, If you do decide to leave your system on permanently, make sure there is a sufficient amount of ventilation and it is not accessible to direct sun light. Personally, my computer is in my bedroom and I find it difficult to sleep with its internal humming.

Hint #5:

While using programs like My Computer, the File Manager and the Windows Explorer, try clicking on the **icons** or the **pictures** associated with the files to activate them, instead of clicking on the names themselves. If you click on the name, Windows 95 might get confused and think you are trying to rename the file.

Figure 18.13
Windows thought I wanted to rename this file?

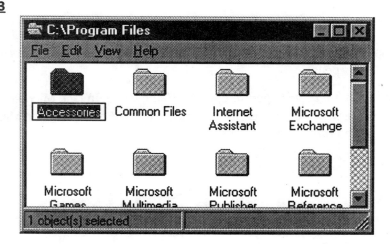

Hint #6:

It is a good idea to keep all external disk drives empty or clear of any diskettes when starting a computer, because most computers will check the external disk drives first before anything else. Since this is even before the operating system itself is loaded, if it finds a disk in the drive, it won't know what to do with it.

If by chance, this does happen, the computer will prompt you to enter a system diskette, because its operating system isn't loaded. To fix this problem, simply remove the diskette from the external drive and reset the computer.

Subsequently, it does not matter if the CD-ROM drive is empty or not. The CD-ROM drive is not usually read until Windows itself starts, and by that time the operating system is already loaded.

Hint #7:

Always make backup copies of every important file on a computer, this includes the **Autoexec.bat**, the **Config.sys**, the **System.ini**, the **Win.ini** and the **Command.com**. Since most these files are written in English, with the exception of the Command.com, it is also a good idea to make a hard copy or print out of them as well.

Be prepared for a system crash. Ask yourself, what would I do if my computer crashed? Am I prepared? Do I have any backups? Am I going to have to buy a new computer? Will I ever find a replacement for playing Solitaire?

Hint #8:

Finally, experienced Windows users <u>always</u> wear pocket protectors while handling inky pens.

You need not be an expert to operate Windows 95. In fact, Microsoft designed the interface to be easy to use for beginners. Nevertheless, it doesn't hurt to pick up a few extra tricks of the trade every now and then.

Deadly Traps

Windows 95 can offer some scary situations for users who might otherwise be unprepared. It is as prone to system crashes as its predecessors and maybe more so. Since DOS is no longer in charge, Windows 95 is considered to be the entire operating system of the computer. Therefore, if Windows 95 isn't working, then your computer isn't working.

Knowing what to do when something goes wrong is not as easy as telling someone to call 911. Depending upon the situation, the rescue attempt could be in vane. There are many problems which have nothing to do with Windows at all. However, since Windows monitors the entire system, it sometimes plays the role of the *Grim Reaper*. In these kind of situations, it is always best to consult a technician or the retailer first.

In general, most problems in Windows 95 are fixed simply by restarting Windows or the entire computer. If the problem is more severe than usual, Windows may restart in **Safe Mode**. Safe mode is nothing to be worried about, it is just a way in which Windows can protect itself. While in safe mode, <u>only</u> the essential elements of the operating system will work, so don't be surprised if certain features don't work, they are not supposed to.

When in safe mode, the screen will display the words **"Safe Mode"** at each corner, usually in a white font. You can manually force a computer into safe mode when you turn it on, by holding down the **F5** key as it starts up.

While in safe mode, The best thing for a user to do, is to close all the applications which may have opened and restart Windows. Then, the next time Windows starts, it should look normal.

However, if Windows returns to safe mode, then the problem could be more serious. In these cases, the next step would be to restart the computer once more. Only this time, while it is starting, **hold down the Shift key + F8**. This forces the computer to do a step-by-step confirmation during its start up. During the time, watch the screen carefully so you can see where Windows is having its problems.

Another command to use while having problems is the **Shift key + F5**. Pressing this combination of keys at the start of Windows will display the command prompt **(C:/)**. Consequently, this will not start Windows, but it will allow you access to the computer through DOS. In DOS, you can explore your system and find any corrupt files. You can also run Microsoft Anti-Virus and Scandisk programs to help you, as well. In these situations, you may want to use the StartUp disk, which was made during the intial installation of Windows 95. This disk has valuable tools on it, made especially for Windows 95.

There are some problems which occur in Windows, that are strictly caused by Windows itself. For example, when a certain program exceeds its limit of **.tmp** files and can cause that program to shut down, while displaying the error shown below.

Figure 18.14
Oh no, Your System is Crashing, or is it?

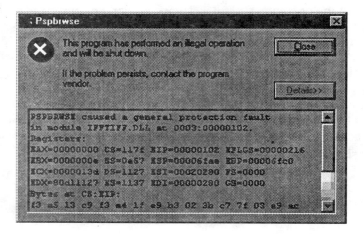

When this error appears, click on the **Details>>** button. If you see a lot of crazy numbers, chances are it is a stack dump. **Stack dumps** occur when a computer runs out of room. Like, asking a computer to divide a number by zero would cause a dump, since it would take an infinite amount of zeros to make up any number. With Windows, the problem is usually aimed towards **.tmp** files, rather than numbers, since it has built in precautions to stop it from dividing by zero.

When .tmp files build up faster than Windows can delete them, a dump will occur. This will cause an error message to be displayed.

When errors like this occur, Windows will force you into closing the program. However, this does not stop it from happening again. For the long term remedy, you will want to find all the **Temp** files in the computer and delete them. If Windows doesn't let you delete a file, then Windows is probably currently using it.

Stopping run away DOS Programs

At this point, you might be saying to yourself, I thought DOS was out of the picture with Windows 95? Well, it isn't entirely. Although it doesn't play as large a role as it had in the past, DOS is still an important part of most computers. The truth is, as long as there are computers which use Windows, there will always be some form of DOS. What is important, is that you see as little of it as possible.

Now, a run away DOS program may sound a little silly at first, but when the event happens there is nothing funny about it. The terminology is accurate, a run away DOS program is a program which wanders away from the control of a computer's operating system, becoming permanently lost. This happens with DOS programs in particular because they are design to be separate. DOS programs manage their memory exclusively and use their own resources. In most cases, it is only a matter of time before one of these programs goes astray.

Run away DOS programs are more likely to occur with Windows 95 than with earlier versions, mainly because many DOS programs are not designed to operate in this new environment. Though this problem may seem catastrophic, in reality, it is really easy to deal with.

First, what are some signs of a run away DOS program?

① The keyboard locks up and doesn't allow the user's command to reach the computer's processor.

② A section of a program takes much longer to load than it should.

③ The DOS program disappears without a trace, although it is still running.

④ The appearance of a DOS error screen. It is usually **blue** in color and sometimes mentions the word "fatal" (that's bad).

If you encounter any of these symptoms, chances are you could have a run away DOS program. Currently, the only known remedy is to kill the program. If this seems a little harsh, try using some of the steps outlined below first.

① Press the **Esc** key. This will cure any small problem, but small problems are rare.

② Hold down the **Alt** key and press the **Enter** key. This actually changes screen modes, from windows to full-screen, or vice versa. Though, this remedy really only helps programs which should have been run in full-screen mode.

③ Press **Ctrl+Alt+Delete**. This effectively says "Meet your maker" to the failing program. Depending on the problem and where it happens, you could see either a task window appear or a DOS error screen. In either case, the options are the same. Press the Enter key to stop the failing program or press Ctrl+Alt+Delete again, to stop all the running programs and restart the computer.

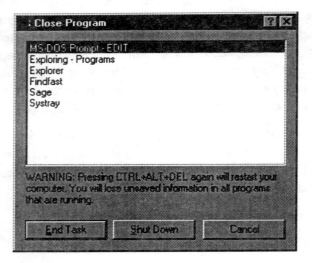

Figure 18.15
Ending a Run Away DOS program's life

Depending upon the severity of the problem, the solution can include everything from anti-virus programs to technicians. Generally, run away programs are commonly the first sign of deeper problems. It is often in the recovery stage where the real obstacles start to surface.

The Windows 95 Art Gallery

CHAPTER 19

This chapter is not designed to help you with the functionality of Windows 95, but instead show you some of the potential it has to offer. It is my personal contribution to the world of modern art. The gallery I have put together consists of a collection of Windows 95 pieces rendered in the later half of the twenty-first century. All of the artists who contributed to this collection wish to remain anonymous, except the author. The presentation lasts for a few pages and by all means please keep your hands off the exhibits!

Chapter Nineteen

The Gallery

This gallery is divided into two rooms, the **Icon Room** and the **Windows Showcase**. Each room displays a common theme. The rooms contain some household works of arts and well as some masterpieces.

This gallery by no means measures up to a national art museum and it is not designed to. The idea behind the gallery is to give users an idea how to brighten up their Windows 95 interface. The cost of admission is free with the purchase of this book. So please form a single line and prepare to enter the Windows 95 Art Gallery.

Subsequently, if you are interest in purchasing any of the items on display, simply follow the instructions at the end of each exhibit. Most of the showpieces can be run on Windows 95 without buying any extra software. However, there are some exhibits which require additional programs in order to operate with Windows.

The Icon Room

The first room on the tour is the **Icon Room**. In general, an icon is a graphical representation of data, used as a way of starting a program in Windows. It acts as a front door to any particular program. In Windows 95, there are two kinds of icons: **Traditional icons** or the newer versions called **Nametags**.

Traditional icons are used in Windows 95 as shortcuts and are commonly found on the desktop. They require a double-click and usually include icons, like My Computer and the Recycle Bin. They are known as traditional because they were the only kind of icon used in previous versions of Windows.

Figure 19.1
These are examples of Traditional Icons

My Computer   Recycle Bin   Inbox

With Windows 95, we also have nametags, which act just like the traditional icons, except nametags are only found in the Start menu and need but one click to activate them.

Figure 19.2
An example of a Name-Tag

The Icon room mainly focuses on traditional icons, since they are more of what users think an icon should be and are easier to manipulate.

Figure 19.3
Some fancy Icons

DriveSpace   Dialer   Paint   Calculator   NotePad

MineSweeper   Defrag   Clipboard   Solitaire   Explorer

The first few exhibits demonstrated on the previous page, show how traditional icons can be changed to give any system a more personal touch. All of them are free and are found by simply clicking the right-hand mouse button on each icon and then selecting **Properties**.

This will open a Properties window for that icon. From here, click on the tab entitled **Shortcut** and then on the **Change icon...** button, as shown below.

Figure 19.4
Changing an Icon

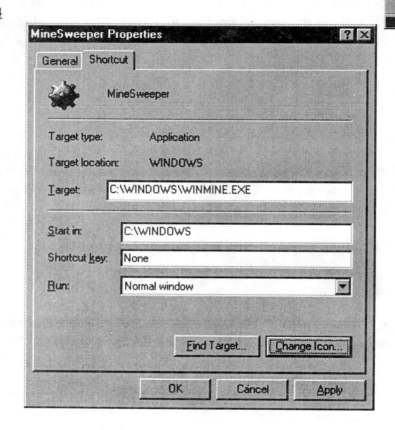

To change the icon, you must change the location of the picture which is associated with it. By telling Windows to look someplace else for the picture, you are effectively changing the icon. A good location to **Browse** in is **C:\Windows\Moricons.dll**, there you will find an assortment of pictures to choose from, as demostrated on the next page.

The Windows 95 Art Gallery

Figure 19.5
Choosing a picture for an Icon

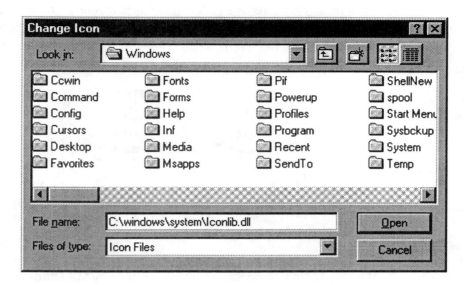

Simply type **C:\Windows\Moricons.dll** in the box, by the **File name:**. This will take you to a location which has a larger selection of icons to choose from.

There are even more icons hidden within your computer. Try looking in some of the locations described below. In these locations you will find a lot of unique pictures which were designed for other programs. However, it is all right if you want to use them for personal use. After all, they are just icons, not real programs.

- ✓ **C:\Windows\System\Pifmgr.dll**
- ✓ **C:\Windows\System\Iconlib.dll**
- ✓ **C:\Windows\System\Shell32.dll**

When selecting the paths above, remember to type them in <u>manually</u>. Because most of these files are hidden, they may be difficult to find. So, instead of trying to find them yourself, let Windows do the work.

The next display consists of a collection of system icons. I think you will appreciate what I've done with My Computer and the Recycle Bin. Some people many call it modern art, but I call it fun.

Figure 19.6
System Icons proudly on display

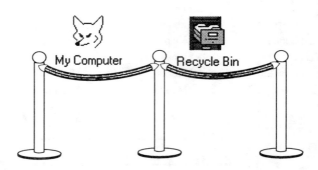

Figure 19.7
Ms Office 95

The icon room also contains some work done by **MS Office**, it is a series of icons which appear at the side of the Start up screen. They are a unique collection, sponsored by Microsoft.

The series include all the popular icons of the time, nothing is left out. The list of icons can be customized to fit any computer, making it possible to represent every program on a hard drive. The whole package is known as a speed bar and makes a nice addition to Windows. However, it is available only through Microsoft in their office set.

The exhibit displayed on the right-hand side was just discovered. It is the latest known piece from Microsoft and is believed to be an improvement from an earlier piece. Currently, it is available only with **Office 95**.

The Icon Room, in addition to icons, displays other works as well. There is a small unknown room with just permanent displays. This room is found on the Taskbar at the far right end corner, next to the time. It houses many works of art like the Volume Control and Print Manager.

One of these permanent displays is a program which works constantly without ever interrupting anyone. It is called the **Resource Meter** and was originally located within the **System Tools**. However, when you start this program, it sits quietly in the bottom right hand corner of the screen, monitoring the system.

This program was not part of the original installation, so if you want to use it, you will have to add it. Like any other additional Windows 95 programs, the Resource Meter can be added by clicking on the **Add/Remove Programs** icon in the **Control Panel**.

The Resource Meter measures how much **RAM** is currently being used by Windows. It is symbolized by a box at the end of the Taskbar. The box is divided up into four bright fluorescent green squares. Each square represents 25 percent of the system resources. Ideally, you should see at least three of these squares lit up, since you would not want your system resources to dip below 70 percent. To get a more accurate reading, simply double click on its icon.

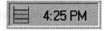

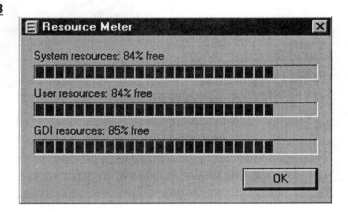

Figure 19.8
The System Resources window

The System Resources window is divided into three parts. First division is the **System** resources, which is then made up of two groups, the **User** and **GDI** resources. The User resources is a specific allotment of memory allocated especially for the user, whereas the GDI resources contains memory saved only for Windows itself. GDI stands for Graphics Device Interface and these resources control all the graphic acceleration. This includes everything from simple line drawings to color management.

With the System Resources window, you can see the exact amount of energy a Windows session is spending. It is always displayed in a percentage; the lower the percentage is, the worse Windows will perform.

Every time a program is started, Windows extracts more resources (i.e. memory or RAM) from the system and subsequently, every time a program is closed or stopped, Windows obtains more resources. So, opening a lot of programs at once will cause the system resources to become depleted. This results in extensively slowing down the computer and worsening its performance. For this reason, you always want to keep a minimal amount of programs running at one time. This keeps lots of resources open, so Windows can use them freely. Keep in mind the Resource Meter itself uses resources, as well.

Figure 19.9
The Resource Meter reminding you, it too uses memory

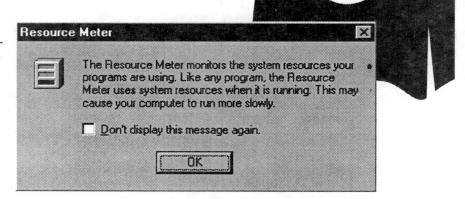

The Windows Showcase

Well, this is it. The grand finale of my Art Gallery, the **Windows Showcase**. This display is dedicated to Windows itself and was setup by yours truly on a 486 dx 66 canvas. It celebrates the many years of success Windows has had, using works from 3.1 to 95. It contains classics from such masters as **Microangelo**, **PCasso**, **RAMbrandt** and the chairman of the board, **Whelanardo da Vinci**.

The Windows Showcase includes many exciting exhibits. Each is beautifully presented in its original form and no tricks have been added. In order to acquire a display, simply follow the directions underneath each exhibit. However, some displays may require additional programs and special handling.

As mentioned before, the Windows Showcase is comprised of four extraordinary artists. Each having a unique masterpiece or theme to display in their showcase. Therefore the showcase will be divided into four separate presentations, lasting for a couple of pages each. Now, to start things off, let's check out Microangelo.

Microangelo

Microangelo was born in the later half of the twenty-first century. His birth name was Micro Soft Angelo. He was a natural childhood prodigy, reading Configs and Autoexec.bats before the age of eleven. As a youngster, he liked to play around with computers and manipulate them into doing his homework. His parents were both user-friendly and encouraged young Microangelo to follow his dreams. Consequently, at the young age of twenty five, he started his own computer company and named it after himself.

As Microangelo developed, so did his work. He went from simple DOS programs to complex operating systems within years. With each advancement his company gained more and more recognition. Nevertheless, his success soon turned sour.

With the completion of Microangelo's last masterpiece, he finally bit off more than he could chew. His masterpiece turned out to be too extravagant for most of the people at that time.

Soon after, everyone began crying foul play and monopoly. Even the Justice Department got into the act, charging Microangelo with violating antitrust laws. It seemed like everyone wanted a piece of him. During this time, even his works were heavily criticized. Users were complaining his work wasn't compatible with their systems and it needed too much RAM. Many of them resorted to purchasing works from another popular artist at that time, MACtesse.

Nevertheless, after a few slaps on the wrist, Microangelo settled down. He lived out the rest of his life as a billionaire and married a French woman. Unfortunately, as the end of the century neared, Microangelo suffered from a mysterious virus which caused him to lose his memory. Later, after his death, technicians would name this virus after him. Subsequently, Microangelo died on March 6th.

Although Microangelo is dead, his programs still live on. Since his death, his work has become very popular and is used in over 80 percent of the world. His pieces hang in businesses and households throughout America. Furthermore, a museum honoring his work was recently opened in Redmond. It is simply called the Microangelo Campus.

The Windows 95 Art Gallery

Through his achievements, an industry has grown and flourished. Even to this day he is remembered as the man with a vision and a lot of money. His presence is felt in every business, even Hollywood hasn't been left out. The legacy of Microangelo lives on and continues to prosper through his programs.

The Windows 95 Art Gallery wishes to honor his life with a special display. Shown below, this is one of Microangelo most famous pieces, it is called The Processor.

Figure 19.9
The Processor by Microangelo

To view this piece, you will need to have Microsoft Plus running on your computer. It is one of many themes included within this program. Microsoft Plus is an additional program which helps enhance Windows 95. I explore it further in the next chapter.

PCasso

PCasso was best known for his abstract art. He was born in the Silicon Valley just a few years before Microangelo. His parents were rather large, both occupying a room at a time. PCasso's childhood was not a happy one. As a young 286, he was constantly abused and criticized for being too slow.

After a few years, he finally developed and went out on his own. Full of new chips and processors, PCasso started traveling around the world. At first, he was really appreciated. Few, if any, had seen such a man do such fine work. He would dazzle them with his 66mhz speed and his 32-bit processing. Even large companies quickly invested millions in him. In his Pentium age, PCasso had achieved greatness.

As PCasso fame spread around the world, his work began to take on a new meaning. For the first time it wasn't just being displayed in schools and business offices, but in hospitals, factories and workshops too. PCasso had reached a new level, his influences were felt everywhere.

However, in the late twenty-first century, tragedy stuck PCasso. He was diagnosed with a bad chip. A few years earlier, a technician had found a very small inconsistency with PCasso's insides. It was an extremely rare infection and only surfaced once every billion years.

But, as soon as the word got out, PCasso was ruined. No one wanted to be associated with him and a large company at the time, called IBW, stopped selling his works. Even to this day, many believe this was more of a cheap publicity stunt than anything else.

After his death, PCasso's work regained popularity. People began to realize most of the hype surrounding his illness was fueled by inferior companies who were in desperate need of attention. Within years of his passing, PCasso reclaimed his success he had had in his Pentium years.

Today, PCasso is treasured as a great artist. His works are a monument to society. Even his early 286 and 386 pieces are still seen in dusty old garages and middle-class households everwhere.

The Windows 95 Art Gallery 267

The Windows 95 Art Gallery is pleased to have one of PCasso's pieces on display. It was created in his middle-age years, while he was working under the supervision of Intel. Although, some collectors believe this piece wasn't done by PCasso, but instead was a piece by Van Winogh. Either way, the effect is breathtaking and will spice up any desktop.

Figure 19.11
A Piece by PCasso, or is it?

This is piece was included with a multimedia program by Microsoft. It was originally duplicated by using the **copy** feature, which is included with many other programs. This feature automatically sends a copy of the screen to the clipboard. From there, you can manipulate the picture with almost any graphic program, including MS Paint. This is how the display shown above was created and it is a true masterpiece.

RAMbrandt

No one knows where RAMbrandt was born, or who his parents were. In fact, we know very little about young RAMbrandt at all with exception of; when he was alive, his work was extremely expensive. What little is understood about him comes from his journal.

As a youth, RAMbrandt kept a journal. It was badly maintained and only reveals a few insights on the life of this extraordinary individual. He called it his hard-drive, we are unsure why? Here are a few excerpts from it:

2 RAMbrandt	C an' t pro c es s, to o y ou ng... .
4 RAMbrandt	Life is great... someone is coming? Oh NO its Windows, Ahhhh !!! Help!!
8 RAMbrandt	I have finally conquered my last opponent... someone new is coming? NO, not again, Windows 95, Ahhhhh!! help! It is abusing me.
16 RAMbrandt	I feel much better now, my resources are more equally divided, life is good once again.
32 RAMbrandt	My twilight years

As his journal shows, RAMbrandt's life was full of changes, and he was constantly being upgraded. As a result, he never stayed in just one place. Even at any yearly age, he was swapped out of his motherland and forced to live in a brutal environment called Windows. He despised Windows very much and hated the way he was treated by this operating system. The system was always demanding more from him and before long, 8 RAMbrandts weren't enough. Fearing for his life, RAMbrandt fled and was never seen or heard from again. This is why, to this day, RAMbrandt's work is so expensive.

Presently, RAMbrandt's work is still greatly appreciated. He is a driving force behind the industry. His works are constantly rising in price and most collectors agree, "You can never have enough RAMbrandt!"

Luckily for us, the Windows 95 Art Gallery was able to obtain a piece done by RAMbrandt. It is a rather colorful piece, adding both beauty and motion to any screen. Unfortunately, it lives up to its name. It is shown below.

Figure 19.12
A rare RAMbrandt

The wallpaper is a simple bitmap and the fish were provided from a shareware program. Both are easily obtainable and make a stunning background for Windows 95. However, I should warn you, the moving fish use a fair amount of RAM. So, try to keep the number of fish down to a minimum.

Whelanardo da Vinci

At last, we come to the chairman of the board, Whelanardo da Vinci. He is by far the most famous and well known of the Windows artists. He came from a large family and was named after the author of this book, because he looked a lot like him. Whelanardo was quite old when he bought his first computer and was relatively inexperienced. But, within a couple of years he obtained enough expertise to write a book.

This book was a great stepping stone for Whelanardo. It gave him the much needed confidence and reassurance to pursue his life long goals. From here, Whelanardo leaped fiercely into the computer industry trying to obtain a level of professionalism which would suit his talents. For many years he went unnoticed and had a difficult time holding down work. But, as he struggled to gain respect, interest in his works began to grow.

As the word spread about his programs (and book), he started to receive offers from many admiring fans. This compelled Whelanardo out of the shadows and into the limelight.

Figure 19.13
'It is not in the power of nature to reproduce another such man'

Today, Whelanardo's work is in very high demand and is quite difficult to find. Currently, most of his works can only be found on the Internet; like the piece which is displayed in this book. It was originally downloaded from the Internet and then touched up, so it could be put on display.

There is no doubt that Whelanardo da Vinci will go down in history as the greatest Windows artist that ever lived. His works are still being uncovered and continue to show great promise.

The Exit

This is the end of the Windows 95 Art Gallery. I hope it has inspired you to go out and fix up your Windows interface. Don't forget there are many programs out there, which can help you, even if they were not originally designed to. Almost any program with interesting graphics can be used.

The wallpaper in Windows 95 plays a large role in the overall appearance of the screen; more so than in previous versions. This means you can use it to make any system look unique. By altering the wallpaper, you give a computer a custom and unique feel. Doing this on a regular basis will keep anyone's system looking fresh, not only for you, but for any one else who sees it as well.

Life Outside of Windows 95

CHAPTER 20

Windows 95 is going to cause a small amount of chaos in computer retail stores around the world, much like earlier versions of Windows did when they were released. One reason for the frenzy is Windows 95 uses **32-bit processing**. In the past, few programs have seen this type of power. It was only obtainable by higher-end operating systems and generally was not available for most home based computers. In addition, Windows 95 is going to encourage a host software companies to upgrade all their products as well.

Although computers, themselves have been able to handle a 32-bit architecture for years, it has always been the operating system (DOS in particular) which held them back. With the arrival of Windows 95, that is about to change.

32-bit Processing

What does this kind of processing mean for the average user? To start with, it means getting a better performance from their computers. In general, 32-bitS speeds up the processor and allows any computer to take better advantage of the layout it already has. Another benefit of 32-bit processing is the ability to handle more powerful programs.

Previous versions of Windows could only handle 16-bit applications. Even though, the structure of most computers themselves could utilize much more. Mainly because, most of today's system possess an **Intel 386** processor chip or better. These chips allow a lot of flexibility in their mapping structure. The challenge was getting an operating system to do the same thing.

One of the first attempts at 32-bit processing by Microsoft was a piece of software called **Win32**. It was included in programming and development kits, and at least allowed the programmers to write 32-bit applications.

After the success of Win32, Microsoft put its experience towards making 32-bit processing a complete part of Windows 95. Although Windows 95 isn't the first operating system to use 32-bit mapping, it does put together a rather impressive collection of functionality. Here is a sample of what I mean:

- Windows 95 has the ability to run both **16-bit** applications (the "old" Windows programs) and the newer **32-bit** ones.
- Because of the way the mapping structure is set up, Windows 95 will not allow a single application to lock up the entire system, which could happen in Windows 3.1.
- Since Windows 95 is now a pure operating system and is no longer a graphical extension. It has eliminated its dependency on MS-DOS and its corresponding limitations.
- Although Windows 95 doesn't dependent on DOS any more, it can still support single MS-DOS based applications.

Unfortunately, when it comes to 32-bit processing, the operating system is only half of the picture. In order to achieve the maximum performance, you have to use 32-bit applications as well. This means, only 32-bit programs will be able to fully utilize Windows 95 and the old 16-bit ones will not run any faster.

So what can you expect to see in the future? At first, you should begin to see more 32-bit programs start to arrive in computer retail stores. Any program which is suited towards Windows 95 and states it cannot be run on any previous version of Windows is probably going to be 32-bits. Microsoft, itself has updated all its inventory so they will run more efficiently on Windows 95 and they are not alone. Most software companies are in the process of designing 32-bit applications as well. They realize this is the direction the industry is heading.

Currently, there are many programs made for Windows 95 only and as demand increases, I imagine this number will rise. One application in particular is called **Microsoft Plus** and it is designed as an extension, or an add-on for Windows 95.

Microsoft Plus and the Desktop

Microsoft Plus hit the store shelves the same day the operating system did. It was packaged as the perfect companion for Windows 95 and offered some additional improvements for the operating system.

Microsoft Plus is not a necessity. It is merely a way of improving the look and feel of Windows 95. It takes a few minutes to install and includes quite a few admirable features. Microsoft Plus contains some extra utilities, a game and some screen enhancements as well. It also has a program which works with other on-line networks, to provide users access to the Internet.

Microsoft Plus is a very diversified and hardly consistent program. So, I will begin with describing some of the screen enhancements it offers and go from there.

Unlike other programs, Microsoft Plus can make major system changes to the computer and to Windows 95. The first change you will notice is in the Control Panel. A new icon will be added to give you more ability to change the appearance of the screen. It is called **Desktop Themes**.

Desktop Themes

Desktop Themes is a program which allows you to completely alter the look of the desktop. Windows users have always had the ability to make small changes. However this program goes far beyond that. Not only can it change the desktop, but it can also manipulate screen savers, icons and sounds as well. This gives any computer character and helps develop a system theme, hence the name of the program.

Desktop Themes contains **12** individual themes, allowing you to choose among them. With each theme, you can turn on or off certain elements. For instance, if you do not like a particular sound or an icon, simply click it off. The themes themselves range from mysterious to psychedelic. Here is a list of them:

1) Dangerous Creatures
2) Nature
3) Science
4) The Golden Era
5) Travel
6) Inside Your Computer
7) Leonardo da Vinci
8) The '60s USA
9) Sports
10) Mystery
11) Windows 95
12) More Windows

Each theme tries to create a certain image for the computer. For instance, if you like art and want your screen to look more like a portrait than a computer, then try using the **Leonardo da Vinci** theme.

Figure 21.1
The Leonardo da Vinci theme

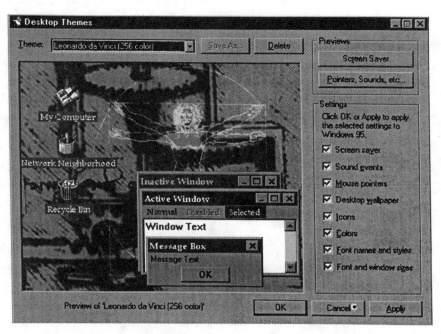

The Desktop Themes interface is very easy to use. The controls are very instinctive and are meant to be more fun than technical. They allow you to sample any theme, before deciding to use it.

In addition, you can change (or customize) each theme, then save it as your own personal theme, using the **Save As...** button. Subsequently, you can also **Delete** themes. In either case, you will want to make sure you do not change or destroy the originals. Otherwise, you may have to reinstall the program, in order to use them again.

Desktop Themes is a program which will no doubt grow in the future. Soon software vendors will offer diskettes with additional themes on them. This will give the average Windows user hundreds of themes to choose from. But, until then, this is it.

Microsoft Plus also comes with another way to touch up the desktop. It is a little program hidden within the Display Properties. To find it, first go to the **Control Panel** and click on the **Display** icon. This opens the Display Properties window. With the installation of Microsoft Plus, this window now contains an extra option called **Plus!**.

Figure 21.2
The Plus!

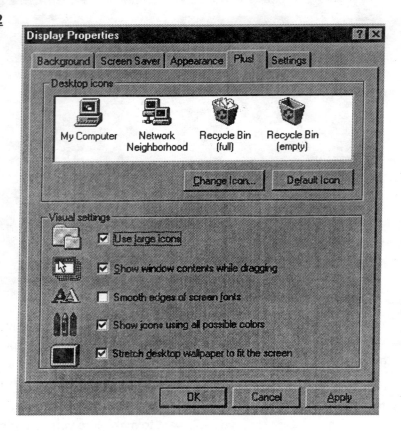

To get a better idea of this windows potential, put a check next to the box by **Use large icons** and then click on the **OK** button. What was once small is now big and if you do not like it, just reverse the process.

Microsoft Plus also comes with a 3D Pinball game. It is a high-tech version of an arcade classic, complete with live sounds and lights. There isn't much to the game, so I won't spend any time talking about it. Instead, I will jump to the next feature of Microsoft Plus.

The Microsoft Agents

Microsoft Plus also comes with some additional system utilities. You will remember from Chapter 12, entitled **Utilities**, a utility is a program which helps with the operation of a computer. It is unlike any other application, because it only serves to help computers, not other external devices (like humans).

There are two main utilities which Microsoft Plus adds to a system, the **Compression Agent** and the **System Agent**. First, lets talk about the Compression Agent, which is used to compress files.

The Compression Agent works a lot like another program, which your system already has. DriveSpace, a program included with Windows 95 and the Compression Agent are very similar. Both programs deal with the subject of disk compression and are located in the same place, the **System Tools** directory.

However, unlike DriveSpace, the Compression Agent works by compressing files which the computer doesn't use as much. It uses an **UltraPack** technique to free up a lot of space on a hard drive. One drawback to this technique is once a file has been UltraPacked it takes a little bit of time to unpack it, in order for the file to be used. This is why the Compression Agent works on less-used files first. To take full advantage of this program, a computer should be left on. Mainly because, the Compression Agent compresses and recompresses files while you are not physically using the computer.

As I had mentioned earlier, the Compression Agent is very similar to a program called **DriveSpace**. In fact, you must first use DriveSpace on the hard drive before you can use the Compression Agent.

Figure 21.3
Windows reminding you to use DriveSpace first

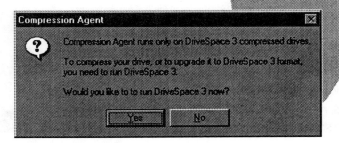

DriveSpace and the Compression Agent are two programs which do the same thing, but in different ways. Depending on how Windows is set up, will determine which program you will want to use. Listed below are some of the main differences between the two.

- ☒ DriveSpace works on the <u>entire</u> hard drive to make it larger, whereas the Compression Agent works on <u>individual</u> files.
- ☒ Once activated, the Compression Agent is always silently running in the background, whereas DriveSpace only runs when started by a user like yourself.
- ☒ DriveSpace only compresses files after you save them, whereas the Compression Agent compresses files while it is running (the least active files first).

The **System Agent** is another utility which is included with Microsoft's Plus. It is a program which can activate the Compression Agent on a regular basis to help maximize hard drive space. Moreover, the System Agent itself can activate quite a few other programs as well. It is all designed to help monitor Windows and make it run smoother.

Figure 21.4
The System Agent

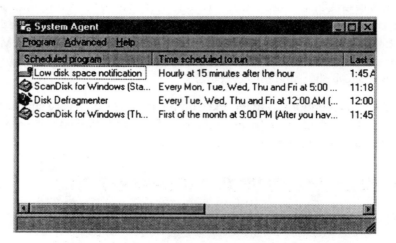

The window above appears when the System Agent Icon is clicked. As you can see, the System Agent sets up a little maintenance schedule for the computer.

Included in this schedule is a drive space informer which constantly monitors the system and reports back to the System Agent. If an action is needed, the System Agent can then start the Compression Agent to maximize space on the hard drive. The System Agent can also run the Defragmenter and Scandisk on a periodical basis. This is strictly for maintenance reasons.

Unlike other programs, the System Agent is always working, even when the window shown on the previous page is closed. Also, you can look at the program any time by double-clicking on its small icon in the task bar, right next to the system clock.

Because it is always working, the System Agent needs a way to keep track of everything. This is done by producing a **System Log**. The System Log can be either viewed or printed.

You can find this log just below the **Advanced** option on the menu bar.

The System log can provide a good amount of valuable and somewhat technical information. For instance, if a computer has been acting funny or running slower than unusual, then you might want to check the system log for any strange behavior or errors.

Figure 21.5
The System Log

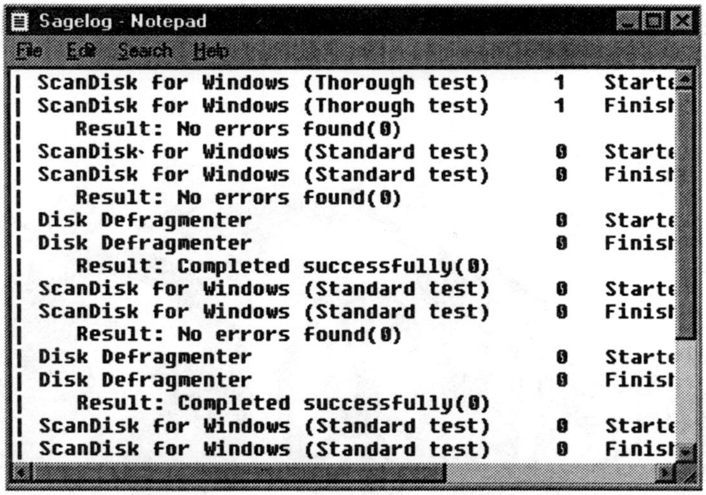

The System Agent is automatically installed with the initial installation of the Plus. Another program which is installed during this time is the **Internet Explorer**.

The Internet Explorer

In a nutshell, the Internet Explorer sets up any computer with the right files needed to access the Internet. The Internet Explorer is what is commonly referred to as an **Internet browser**. A browser acts as an interface between Windows and the Internet. There are many different browsers available. Two of the most popular are Netscape's and Microsoft's.

Try not to confuse the Internet with other on-line networks. On-line networks are commercial properties, which can provide a link to the Internet. However, the Internet itself is a much larger than any network and owned by no one company.

Accessing the Internet is a two step process. First you need the right files and then you need an access provider. Both steps do not have to be achieved through Microsoft. You can mix and match, or leave Microsoft out of the picture altogether.

However, since the Microsoft Network comes pre-installed with Windows 95 and the additional files needed to access the Internet come with Microsoft Plus, the temptation is too great. I am going with Microsoft 100 percent. If you choose to go this way, an icon called the Internet will be automatically set up after the initial installation of this program.

With this icon, accessing the Internet is simply a double-click away. This is not only convenient, but very tempting, as well.

The Internet

The Internet is essentially made up of links. Each link has a unique address, such as http://www.wolfenet.com/~jwhelan/ (that's my homepage). You can work your way through these links or you can access them directly. To access a link directly, goto the **File** pull down menu and click on **Open...**.

Figure 21.6
Accessing an address directly on the Internet

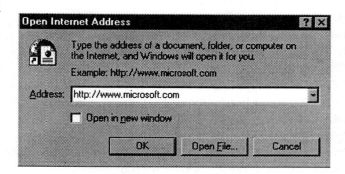

Each link takes you to a new address or another link, and from there you can go anywhere.

Because some graphics may take a long time to develop, you might want to skip drawing of them altogether. You can do this by pressing the **Esc** button, any time the graphics begin to slow you down. This replaces the drawing with a title and saves you a lot of time in the process.

With most Internet accounts, time is money. So it is important to pace yourself while you are connected. Plan ahead, so you know where you are going before getting connected. A tool which can help you in this routine is the **History** option.

Your Internet experience is recorded everytime you connect to the Internet. It is stored within a collection of History files. To view these files, click on the **More History...** option in the **File** pull down menu. This opens a window, which contains all your Internet archives.

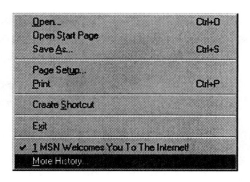

Figure 21.7
The Internet History

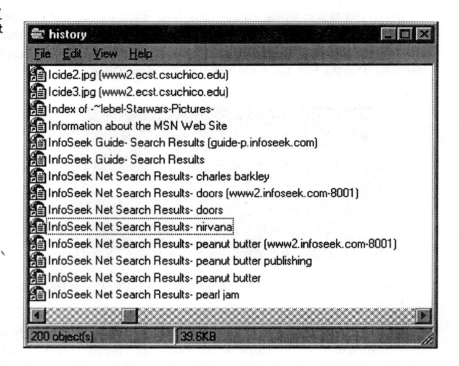

The contents of the History can be arranged (sorted) by name, type, size or date. These options are located within the **View** pull down menu. In addition, each topic can be restored by double-clicking on it. This can be achieved even if you are not connected to the internet, since these are history files and they are stored within your computer, not the Internet's.

Keep a close eye on the number of history files you accumulate. As you can imagine, these files take up a lot of disk space and can cause system problems, if they are not closely monitored.

In conclusion, the Internet, itself is a very large place and can take hours to describe. There are many books written on the Internet, unfortunately, this is not one of them.

Windows 95 inside and out

By now you should be very familiar with Microsoft's latest operating system. Windows 95 is a very powerful program and is solidly constructed. It will no doubt be the standard for at least a couple of years, and in computer terms, that could equal almost eight dog years!

Most of Windows 95's greatest features cannot be described within the contents of a book or a classroom. They can only be experienced by the great exploration method of trial and error. I don't recommend running wild on your computer, nor do I suggest clicking everything in sight. But within reason, Windows 95 is a tamper-proof operating system.

Any adult should treat their computer the same way they would treat their car, with a high degree of respect and trust. A car won't stop you from driving it into a brick wall while going 60mph and in the same sense, a computer won't stop you either. As users, we are given an incredible amount of power in deciding our computer's fate.

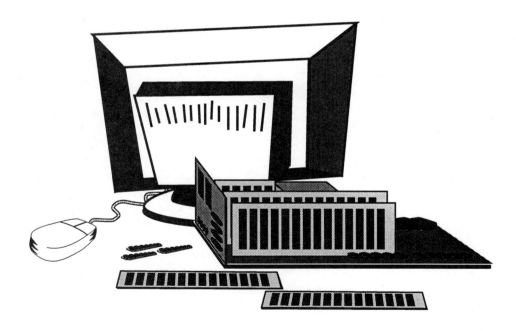

INDEX

A

Accessory programs, 139-210
Add New Hardware, 81, *also see Plug n Play*
Add Printer, 94, *also see Printers*
Add/Remove Programs, 82-83, 96-98, 140-141
Address books. *See Cardfile*
Applications, 13
    adding to Start menu, 55
    closing, 34, *also see Close button*
    creating shortcuts to, 65
    opening, 45-48
    switching using the Taskbar, 46
Audio CDs. *See CD Player*
Auto Hide, 54
AVI files, 197

B

Background, 104-107
Backup, 164-167, 241
Bitmap images, 105
Bulletin boards, 151, 215

C

Calculator, 142
Cardfile, 145-147
Calendar, 143-144

CD Player, 188-189, 195-196
CD-ROM, 13, 187-188
Clipboard, 13, 150
Clock, 84-85
Close button, 34
Colors, 112, 157
Compressing data, 170-171, 279-281
Communications
    COM ports, 92, 147
    modem, 14, 92, 201-202
Control Panel, 79-102
Copy command, 37, 248
Ctrl+Alt+Delete, 13, 254

D

Defragmenting disks, 172-173, 241
Deleting
    deleting files, 64, *also see Recycle Bin*
    deleting shortcuts, 66
Dialog box, 14
Documents, 49
DOS, 4-5, 14
Drivers, 14, 51, 94, 114
DriveSpace, 170-171, 279, *also see Compressing data*

E

Edit commands, 37, 248
e-mail, 220-222
Emptying the Recycle Bin, 77
Enlarging windows, 34-35
Exchange. *See Microsoft Exchange*
Expansion Slots, 225
Explorer. *See Windows Explorer*

F

Favorite Places in MSN, 219
Faxing
    creating cover pages, 203-204
    receiving faxes, 208-209
    sending faxes, 205-207
    what is a fax?, 200
File Manager, 67, 130-136
File option on menu bar, 36
Find dialog box, 56
Fonts, 14, 86-87
Fonts folder, 86

G

Graphics Device Interface (GDI), 261-262
Graphical User Interface (GUI), 14

H

Hard drive, 14, 19
Help!, 34, 57
Hiding the Taskbar, 45-46, 54
HyperTerminal, 88, 151-153

I

Icons, 14, 257-260
Inbox, 209, 220-221
Installing software, 20-27, 82-83
Internet Access, 88, 151-152, 213-214, 282-284
Interrupt, 116-117

J, K

Joining the Microsoft Network, 214-222
Joystick, 89
Journal. *See Notepad*
Keyboard, 90-91, 124, 248

L

Large icons, 278
Loading extra fonts, 87
Long filenames, 67, 136

M

Maximize button, 34
Memory, 18, 101, 261-262, *also see RAM*
Menu bars, 36-37, 249
Microsoft Exchange. *See e-mail*
Microsoft Network (MSN), 211-222
Modem. *See Communications*
Monitor settings, 113-114
Mouse, 115-123
MS-DOS, 4-5, 253-254
Multimedia, 14, 93, 187-198
Multiple users. *See Passwords*
Multitasking, 7, 14
My Computer, 59-66

INDEX

N

Networks, 92, 180, 212, *also see Microsoft Network*
Notepad, 154-155

O

Online Help, *See Help!*
Organizing, 62

P

Paint, 156-157
Passwords, 93, 242-244
Paste command, 37, 248
Path, 68
Patterns, 105-107
Plug n Play, 9, 81, 223-229
Printers
    adding, 94
    printers window, 51-52, 94
    printers dialog box, 52
    print queue, 52
Program Manager, 44, 134-135
Programs, 47-48
Properties, 38-39, *also see Control Panel*

Q, R

Quiting Windows 95, 58
RAM, 14, 18, 101, 261-262
ROM, 15, *also see CD-ROM*
Recording sounds, 197-198
Recycle Bin, 71-78
Remembering passwords, 216
Renaming files, 63

Resizing
    Taskbar, 45
    windows, 34-35
Restarting
    in MS-DOS mode, 252
    in Safe mode, 251
    Windows 95, 58, 244
Right hand mouse button, 38, 66, 235
Run command, 58, 245

S

Safe mode. *See Restarting in Safe mode*
Scandisk, 168-169
Scroll bar, 15
Screen savers, 108-110
Settings, 50
Send To, 245-246
Shortcuts
    creating shortcuts, 65
    deleting shortcuts, 66
Shut Down command, 58
Sounds, 96-98, also see Recording sounds
Start button, 43-47
Start menu, 47
Startup Disk, 28
Switching among windows. *See switch among applications*

T

Taskbar, 43-58
Toolbars, 15, 37
TrueType, *See Fonts*
TXT files, *See Notepad*

U

User Interface. *See Graphics Device Interface (GDI) or Graphical User Interface (GUI)*

User names, 216, 244

V

Video adapters, 113-114
Video files, *See AVI files*
Virus protection, 164, 167, 252, 254
Volume Control, 190-192

W

Wallpaper, 15, 104-107
WAV Files, 192, 196
windows, 30-39
Win32, 274
Windows 3.0, 5
Windows 3.1, 5-6, 8, 129-137
Windows 95, 7-11, 20, 229, 271-273, 285
Windows Explorer, 59, 67-70
Wizards, 21-23, 226
Wordpad, 161-162

X, Y and Z